Watercolor Pencil

Guide and Workbook

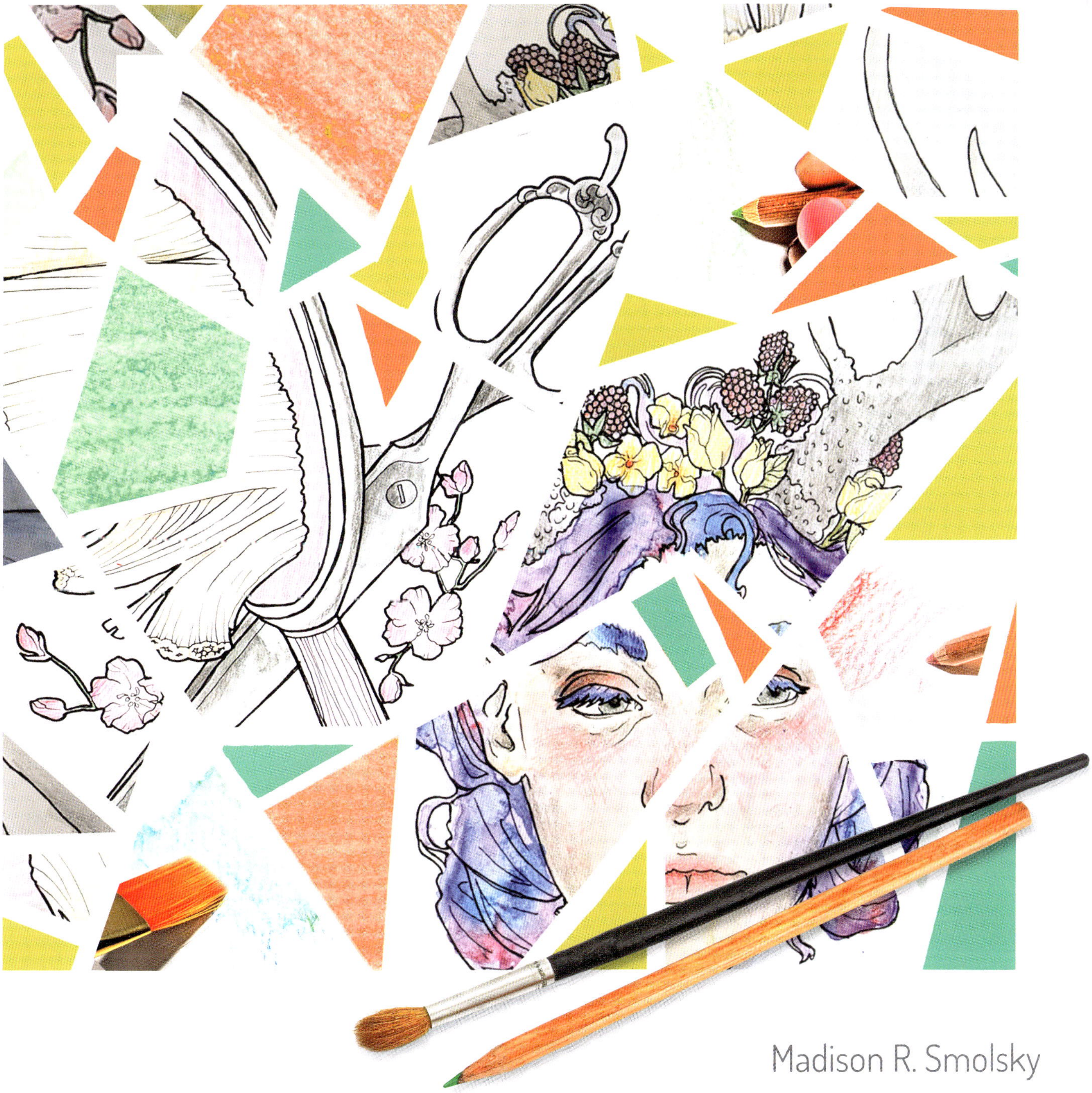

Madison R. Smolsky

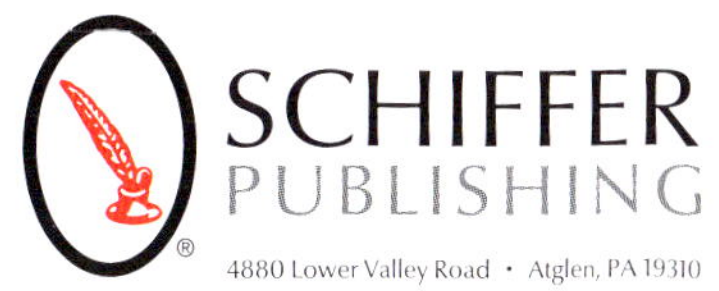

Other Schiffer Books on Related Subjects:
The Painted Word: Mixed Media Lettering Techniques, Caitlin Dundon, ISBN 978-0-7643-5647-6
20 Projects for Alcohol Inks: A Workbook for Creating Your Best Art, Karen Walker, ISBN 978-0-7643-5646-9
Painterly Days—12 Colored Pencils, Kristy Rice, ISBN 978-0-7643-5167-9

Designed by Molly Shields
Cover design by Brenda McCallum
Type set in Tarnished Halo/DIN

ISBN: 978-0-7643-5736-7
Printed in China

Published by Schiffer Publishing, Ltd.
4880 Lower Valley Road
Atglen, PA 19310
Phone: (610) 593-1777; Fax: (610) 593-2002
E-mail: Info@schifferbooks.com
Web: www.schifferbooks.com

Contents

What Are Watercolor Pencils?

What are watercolor pencils? They are much like watercolor pans that come in a palette—watercolor pencils are essentially those pans compressed into a stick. They act as the lead would in a regular pencil. They come in a variety of colors and can be used either as a colored pencil, as watercolors with a brush, or as a combination of the two.

Techniques both for colored pencils and watercolors can be used with watercolor pencils. We will go over a number of these techniques in the following pages.

Lead: the graphite portion in the center of a pencil, which marks the page
Pans: the cubes in which individual watercolor pigments are packaged
Palette: a set of multiple watercolor pans in a variety of colors
Transparent: allowing light to pass through; sheer
Opaque: lacking transparency or translucence

Much like ordinary colored pencils, watercolor pencils come in a variety of colors and quality. Higher-quality watercolor pencils will be easier to layer, allow for a fuller color opacity, be easier to blend with other colors, and be easier to erase. Lower-quality pencils are just as simple to use, but colors will be slightly harder to layer and blend and will remain more transparent (which can be a useful trick when coloring to achieve a glasslike effect).

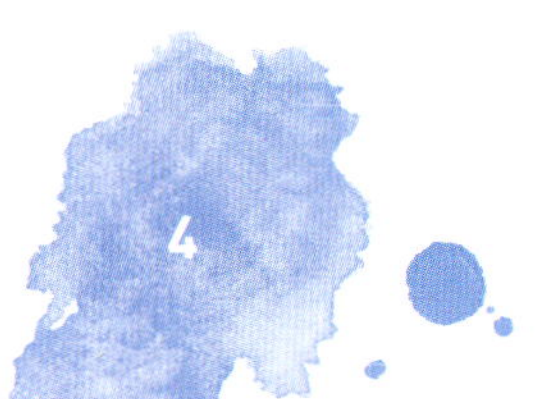

Pencil Techniques

Gradient: Two Ways

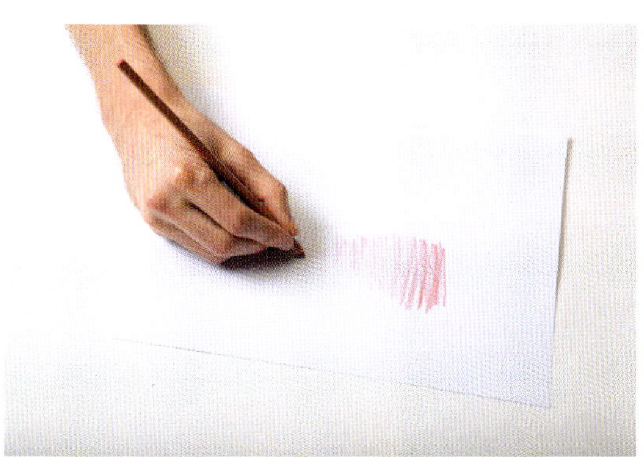

Force

You can achieve a gradient by pressing the pencil harder into the paper to create a darker color while gradually using less pressure to fade the color from the darkest portion to the lightest one.

Layers

Begin with a light layer of color over the area. By adding additional layers, you can build up the saturation and opacity. Gradually lessen the area colored as you add layers.

Shading

Using the gradient techniques, you can achieve a three-dimensional effect. To make something appear three-dimensional, start the gradient at the edge of the image. Starting with the darkest color on the edge that would be farthest away from the light, fade to the lightest color where the most light would be hitting the object.

Depending on the surface, the light can be reflected differently. Metal typically has a harsh change in tones as opposed to a smooth transition. A harsh transition is when the colors are beside each other but there is no blending.

Most other materials can be shaded by using smooth transitions, because they do not reflect the light as extremely. To make an object appear more matte, keep the lightest tone close to the general tone of the object.

To make something appear shiny or glossy, use the same smooth shading as you would for a general object or a matte object. Then apply a harsh highlight of white that follows the curvature of the object.

Your Watercolor Pencils and Water

Watercolor pencils have a broad variety of uses and are more forgiving than either of their counterparts (colored pencils and traditional watercolors). They can be used as colored pencils, as a portable means for watercolor painting, and, more excitingly, as a medium that is somewhere between the two disciplines. As such, there are a few different ways the pencils can be used. In this section, learn how to use your watercolor pencils and the role that water plays.

The pencils can be used two ways in conjunction with water: **directly** and **indirectly**.

Directly

Two Ways

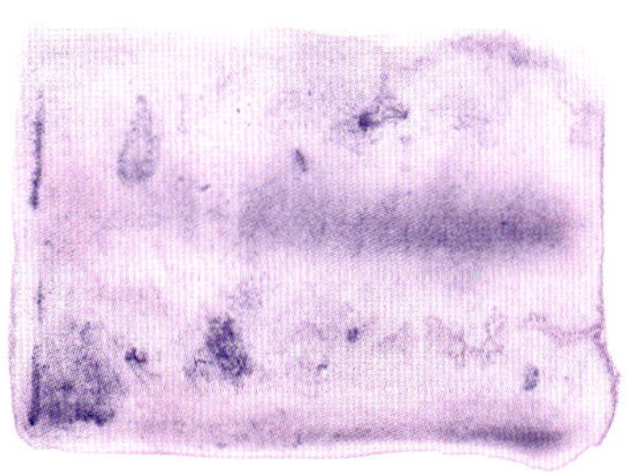

Using the pencil and water directly together will result in more opaque color and allow for finer detail. You can apply the water on the tip of a paintbrush and lightly touch the colored portion of the pencil. This is a good way of getting small amounts of color onto the paper. However, for bigger portions there will need to be a constant reapplication of water, which may not be the best option.

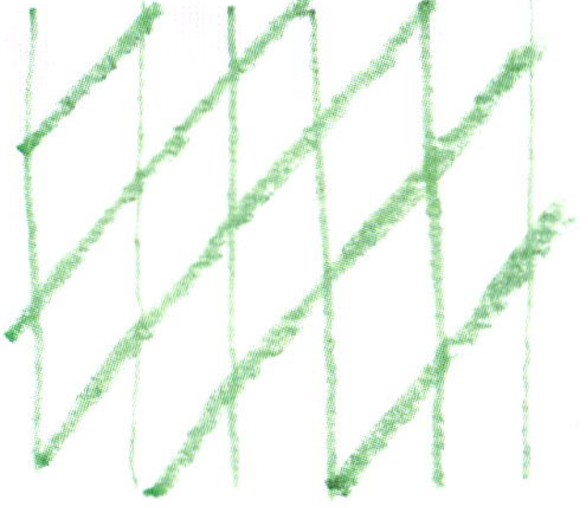

Another way of using the pencil is to dip it into a cup of water, then draw straight onto the paper. This will result in an application that looks more like acrylic paint—an opaque and constant line rather than the softer, less formed application of watercolor.

Indirectly

Three Ways

Using the watercolor pencil as if it were a normal colored pencil, you can color the image fully and use the water afterward to blur the pencil lines to make colors smoother.

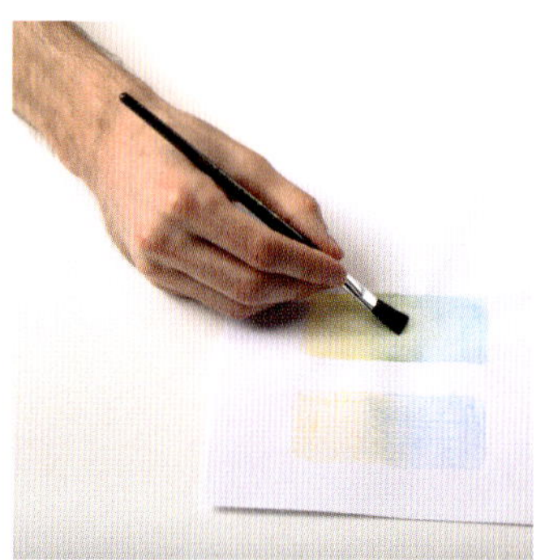

Water can be used as a transitional blending method. By laying down two colors side by side with your dry pencil, then taking a small amount of water on your brush, you can blend the two colors seamlessly. Stroke your brush over the edge of each color until you reach your desired gradient.

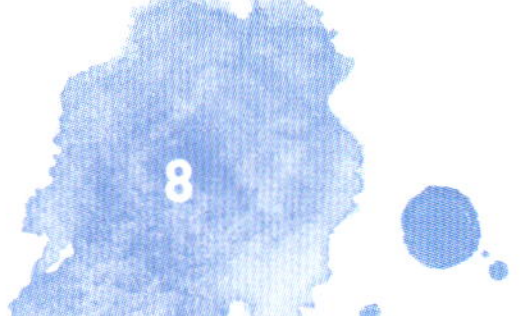

Hint: By combining different methods of water use, you can get a variety of forms, lines, and transitions that will make the images you paint all your own!

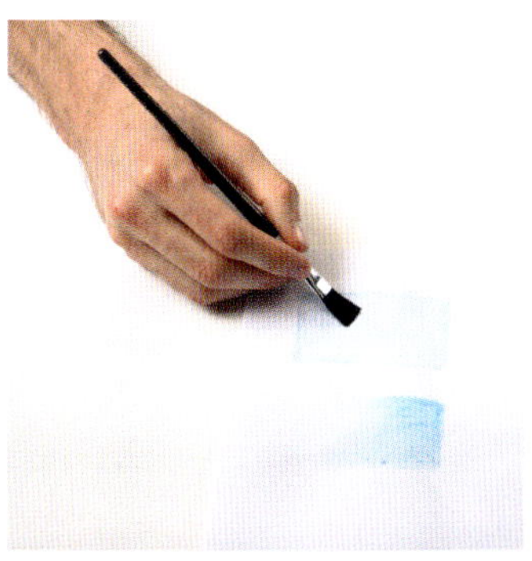

If you want to create an easy shading effect transitioning from a dark tone to light one, lay down color with a dry pencil. After wetting your brush, wipe over the colored portion and gradually move away from it. Adding more water as you go will thin the opacity of the color. To transition from a light color to a darker one, lay down some color lightly, once again hitting it with your wet brush in the opposite direction until you can see that the brush is not pulling any more color. Use the pencil to go over the wet portions of the page, adding color as necessary and using water to blur the lines of the pencil together.

Color Theory: What Is It? And How to Use It

Color theory, in the simplest terms, is the idea that certain colors complement each other or look appealing together. There are three primary colors: red, blue, and yellow. The secondary colors are green, orange, and purple. The complementary combinations are red/green, blue/orange, and yellow/purple. Though it may seem as though these combinations are arbitrary, there is a reasoning behind it. Each primary color is paired with the secondary color that is a combination of the two opposing primary colors. That is, red's secondary color green = blue + yellow; blue's secondary color orange = red + yellow; and yellow's secondary color purple = blue + red.

Now that there is an explanation behind the madness, there is a way to put the theory to good use. You can use any of these color combinations, in any tone, to make colors more vibrant. Knowledge of color theory can be helpful when choosing tones for shadows. Typically, in an object's shadows you want to use the color complementary to that of the object. So, if something is orange or has orange undertones, you would want to use blue in its shadows.

Advanced Techniques

Salt

Salt over watercolor creates a starburst effect as it repels the pigments away from its center. This technique is useful in creating a fabric-like texture on an image or a broken-mirror effect.

Use a wet wash over the page and add pigments in varying locations until you reach your desired level of color opacity. Then sprinkle salt over the image and allow it to dry fully. After it is dry, brush off the salt.

Coffee Grounds

This method is similar to the salt method. However, the paint spreads evenly away from the grounds, in a circular fashion. This is an easy way to create snow or rain falling in an image.

Use a wet wash over the page and add pigments in varying locations until you reach your desired level of color opacity. Then sprinkle coffee grounds over the image and allow it to dry fully. After it is dry, brush off the grounds.

Alcohol

Splattering or dripping rubbing alcohol over a wet wash of watercolor creates a halo effect. Wet the paper to its fullest capacity without soaking through, add your colors, and then take either a dropper or an old brush you do not care for, and gently splatter or drip the alcohol onto the image.

This is an easy way to create a base for jellyfish, create a unique pattern for animal skin, or dilute the pigment in a controlled fashion that gives texture.

Sugar Water

This technique creates a bleeding effect that looks organic and can resemble flowers.

Mix two parts sugar to one part water in a pan over high heat until the sugar is melted. After it is melted, very carefully spread a thin, even layer over the paper. Gently touch a brush with the desired color onto the paper. Be sure to add all desired colors to the paper before the sugar mixture dries. Leave the paper to dry completely before adding ink or anything else on top.

Dry Brushing

On a plastic palette, mix a saturated amount of color from the pencil on the brush with the least amount of water possible. Lightly brush some of the paint off the brush on a paper towel. Then brush over the watercolor paper to bring out the texture of the paper.

Terms to Know

bleed: When pigments spread near or into each other but stay very distinct and do not blend

gradient: The technique of transitioning from one color to another, one shade to another, or one texture to another

hue: A tone of a color that separates it from the rest of that particular color spectrum—for example, orange can be a hue of red or a hue of yellow, depending on which color is more prevalent

layering: Coloring a portion of a page and adding additional color on top to build up opacity or change the hue of a color

lead: The graphite portion in the center of a pencil, which marks the page

matte: Having a quality in which light is not reflected from the surface of an object

opaque: Lacking transparency or translucence

palette: A set of multiple watercolor pans in a variety of colors

pans: The cubes in which individual watercolor pigments are packaged

plastic palette: A plastic tray on which you can mix colors or place paint

shade: A specific color, or darker color in the same color family, which is typically mixed with black

transition: Change from one state to another; usually referring to a change in color

transparent: Allowing light to pass through; sheer

wash: A layer of water over the paper to allow the pigment to spread

light wash: A very light layer of water, where it just barely wets the paper

wet wash: A heavier wash, where the paper is just before the point of being overly saturated

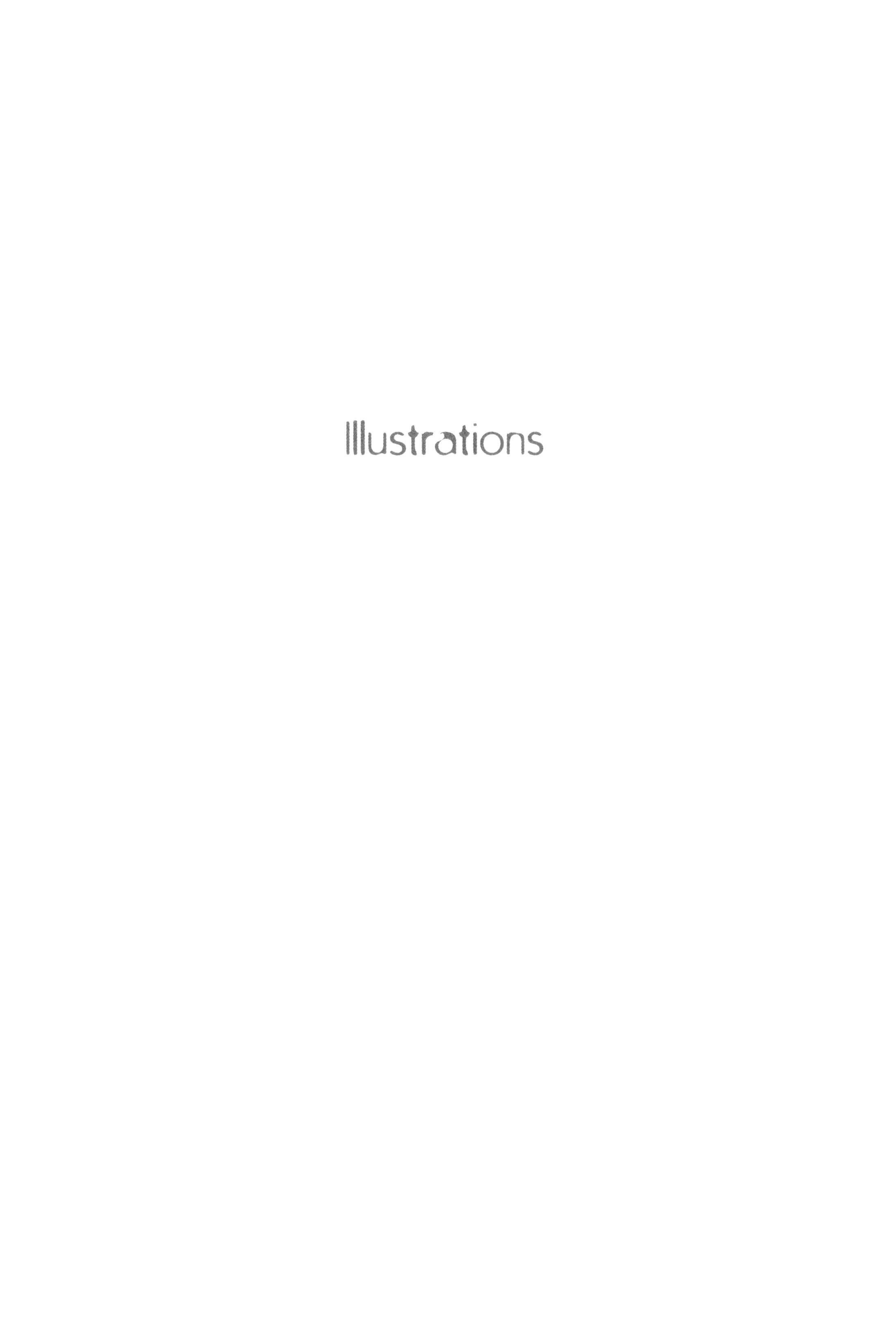

Illustrations

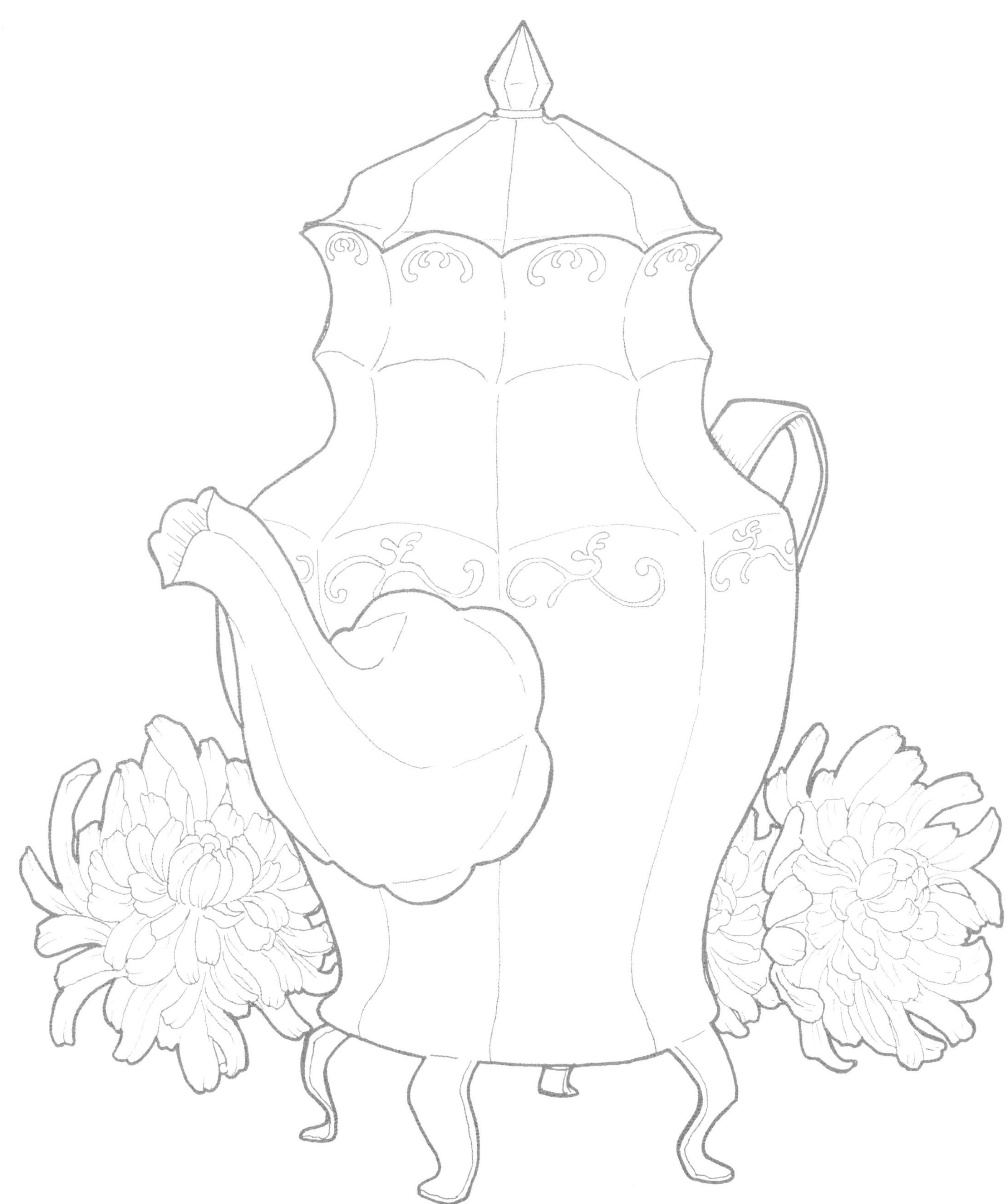

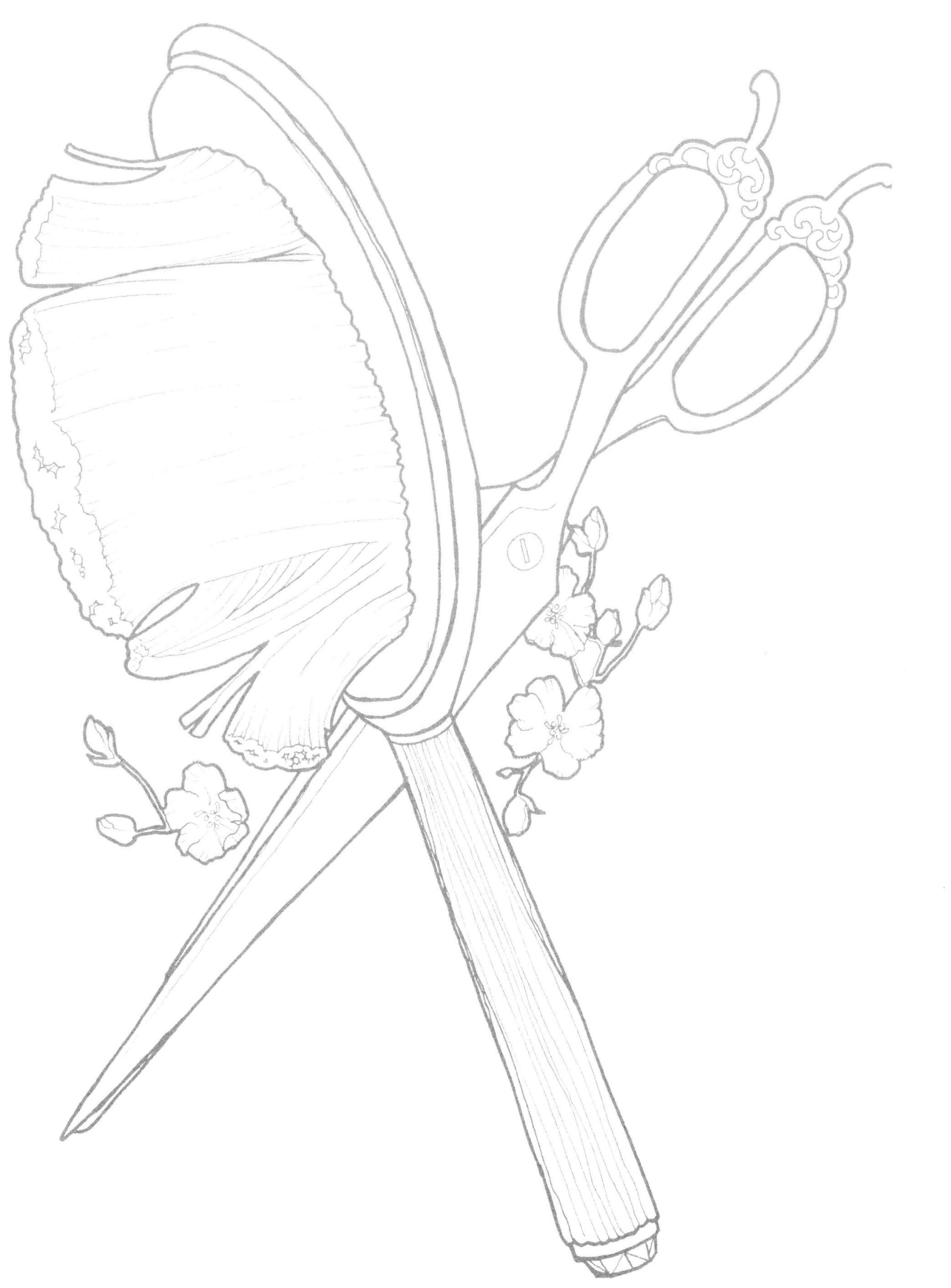

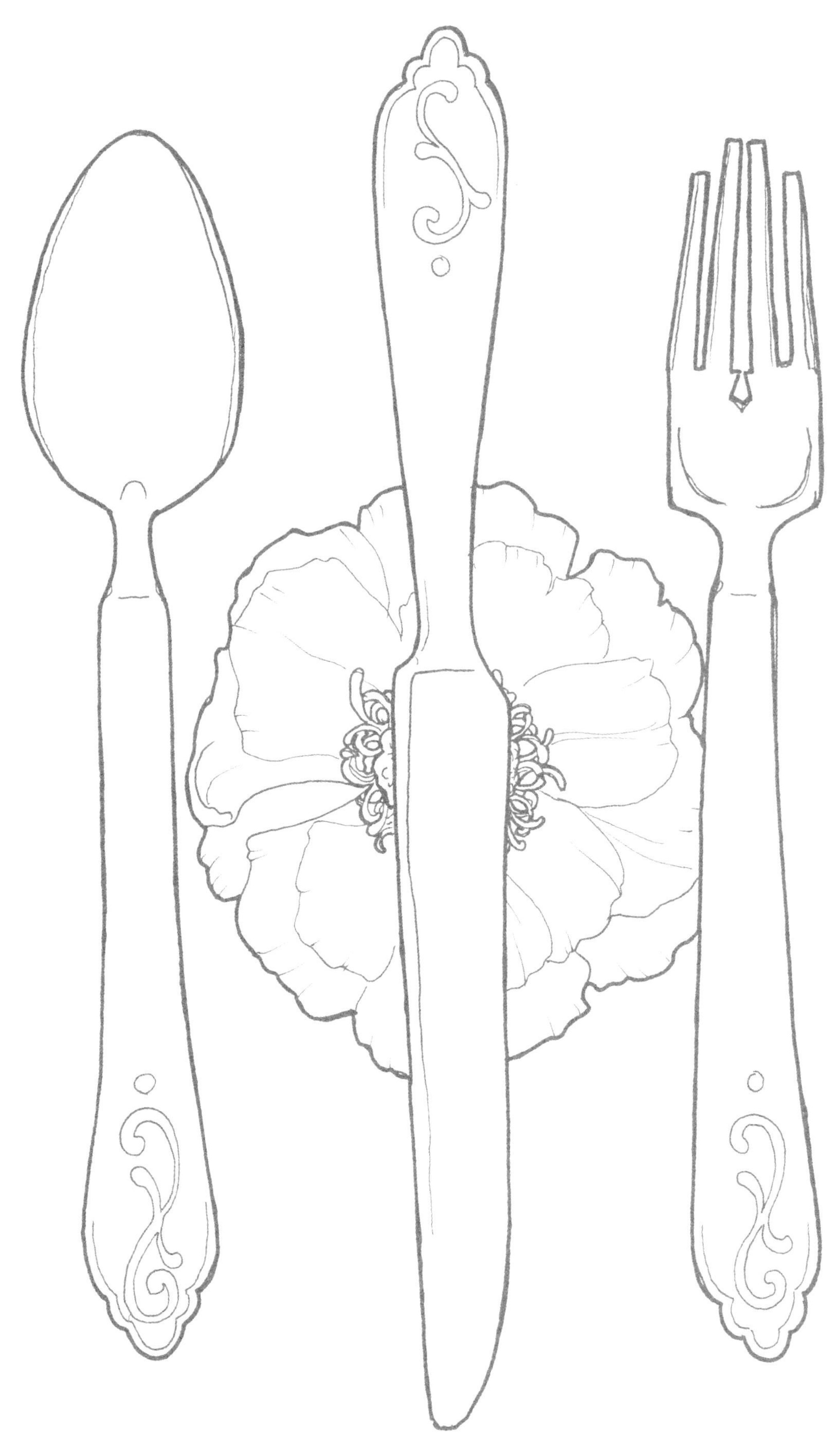

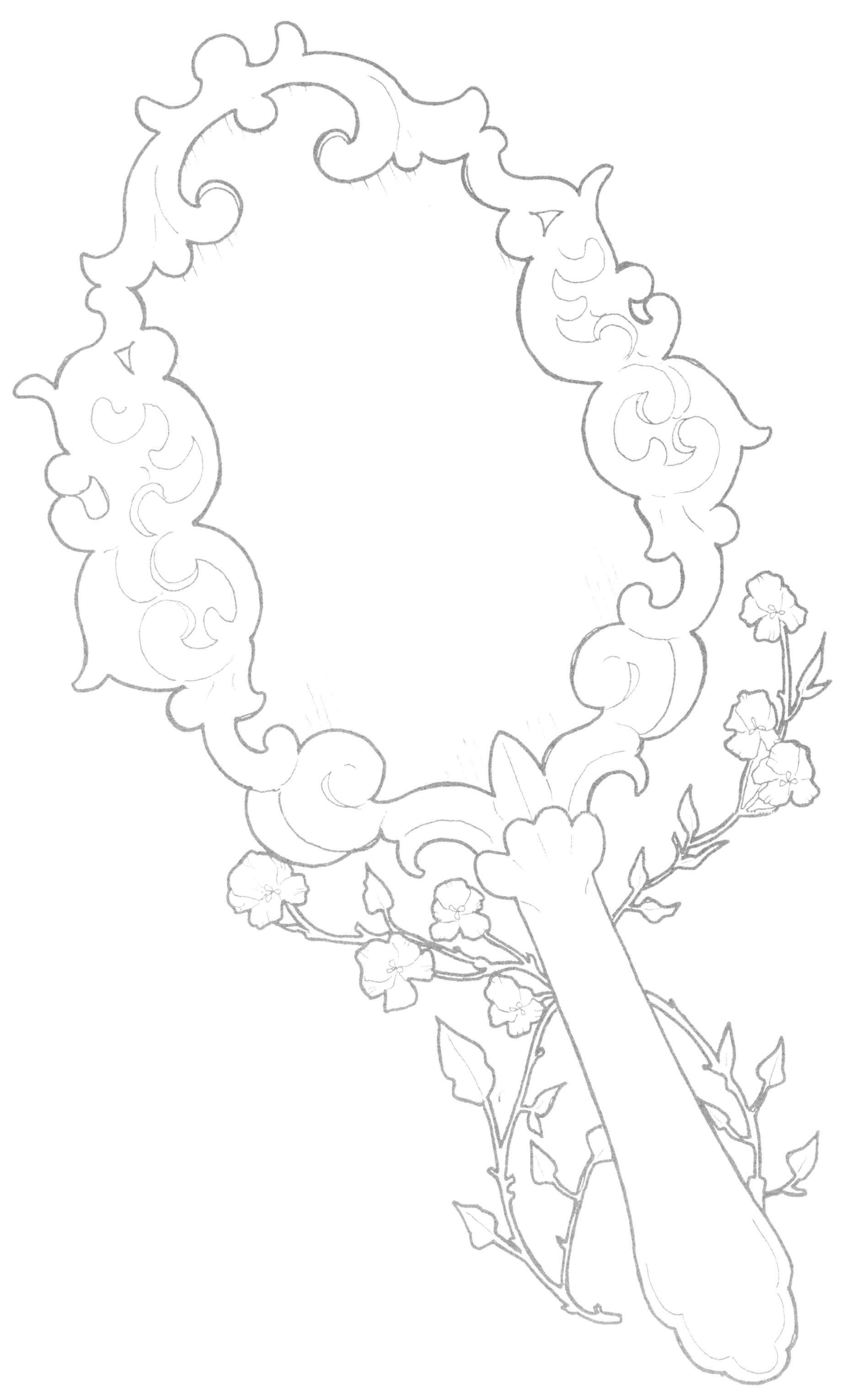

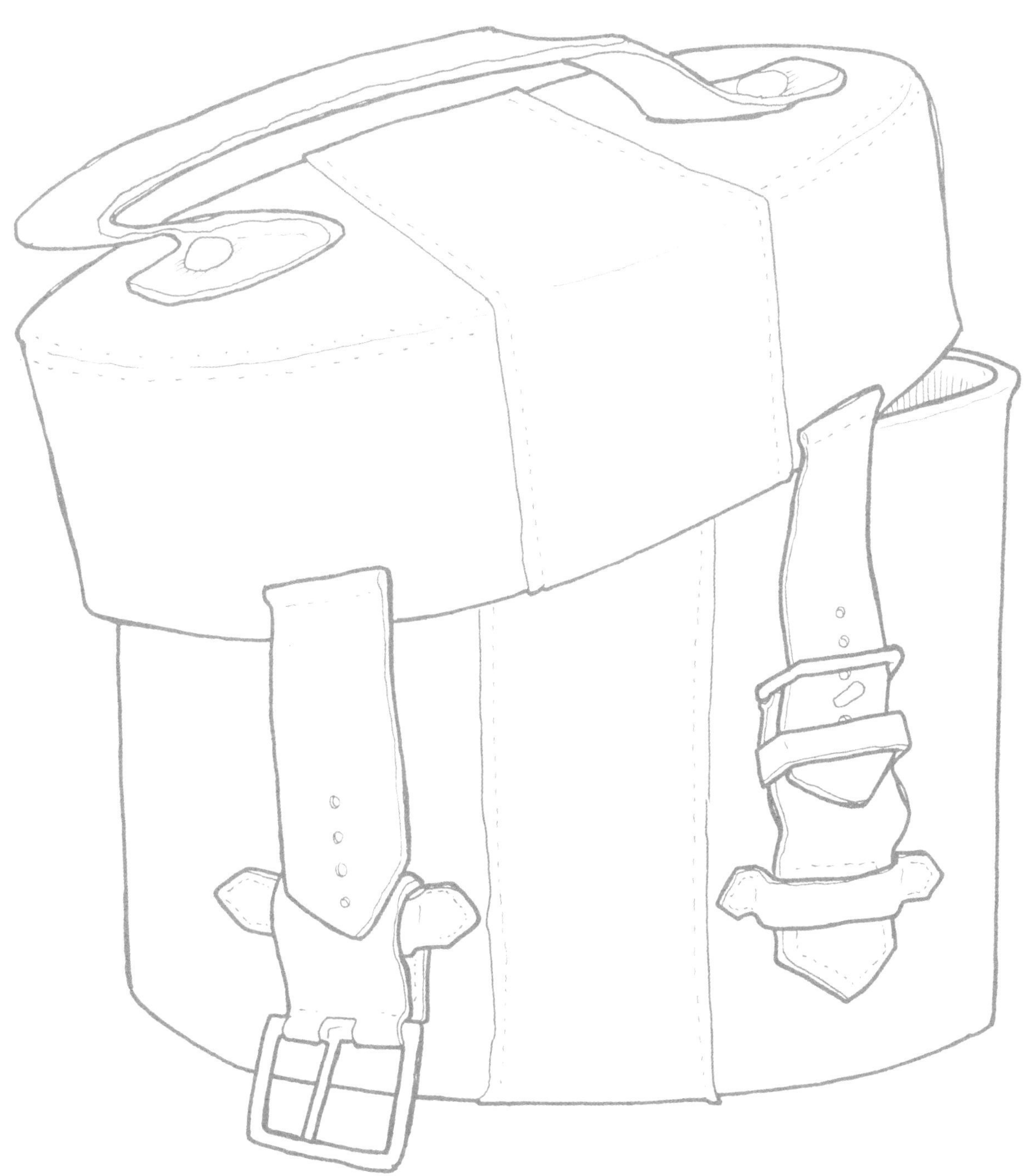

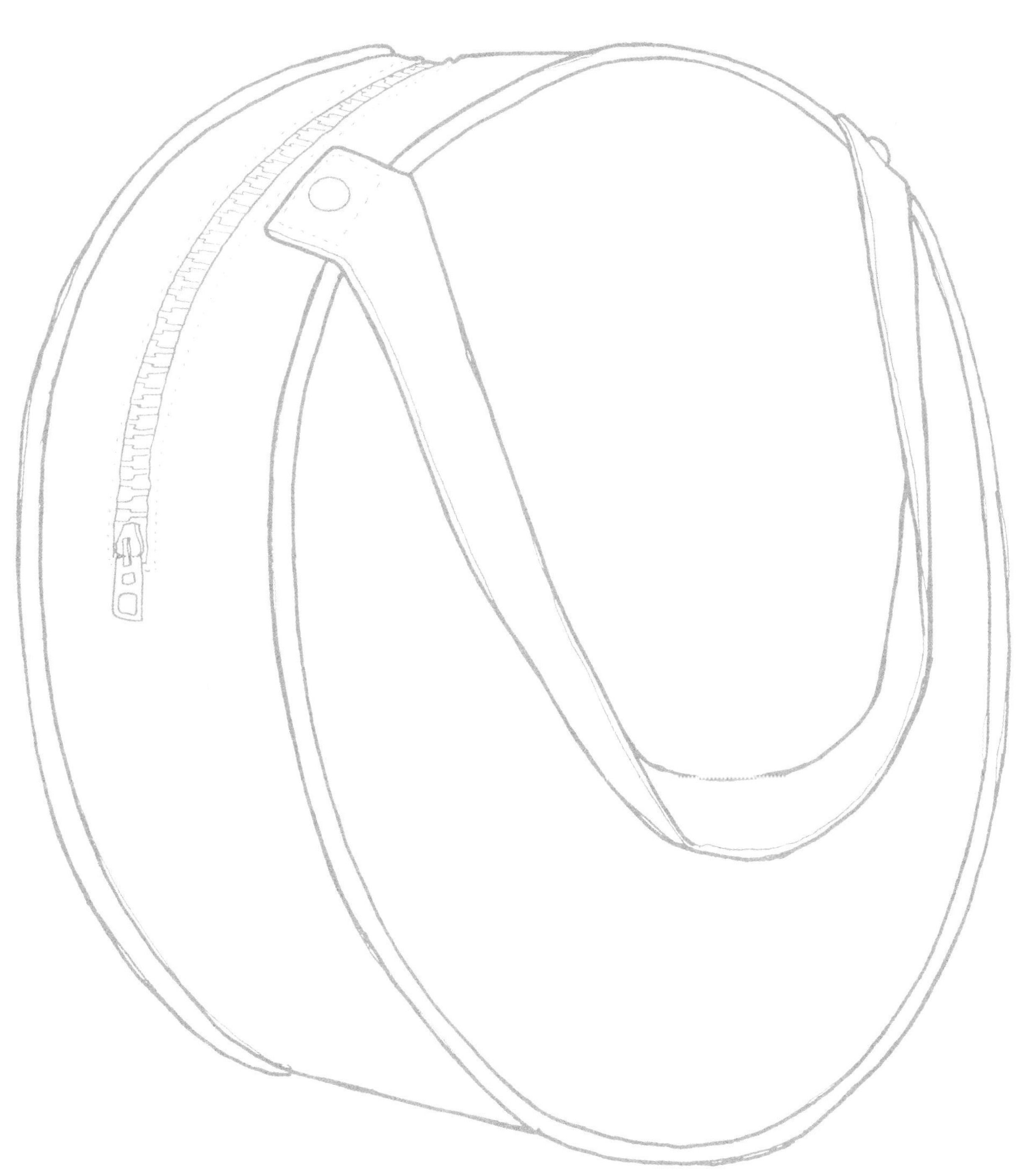

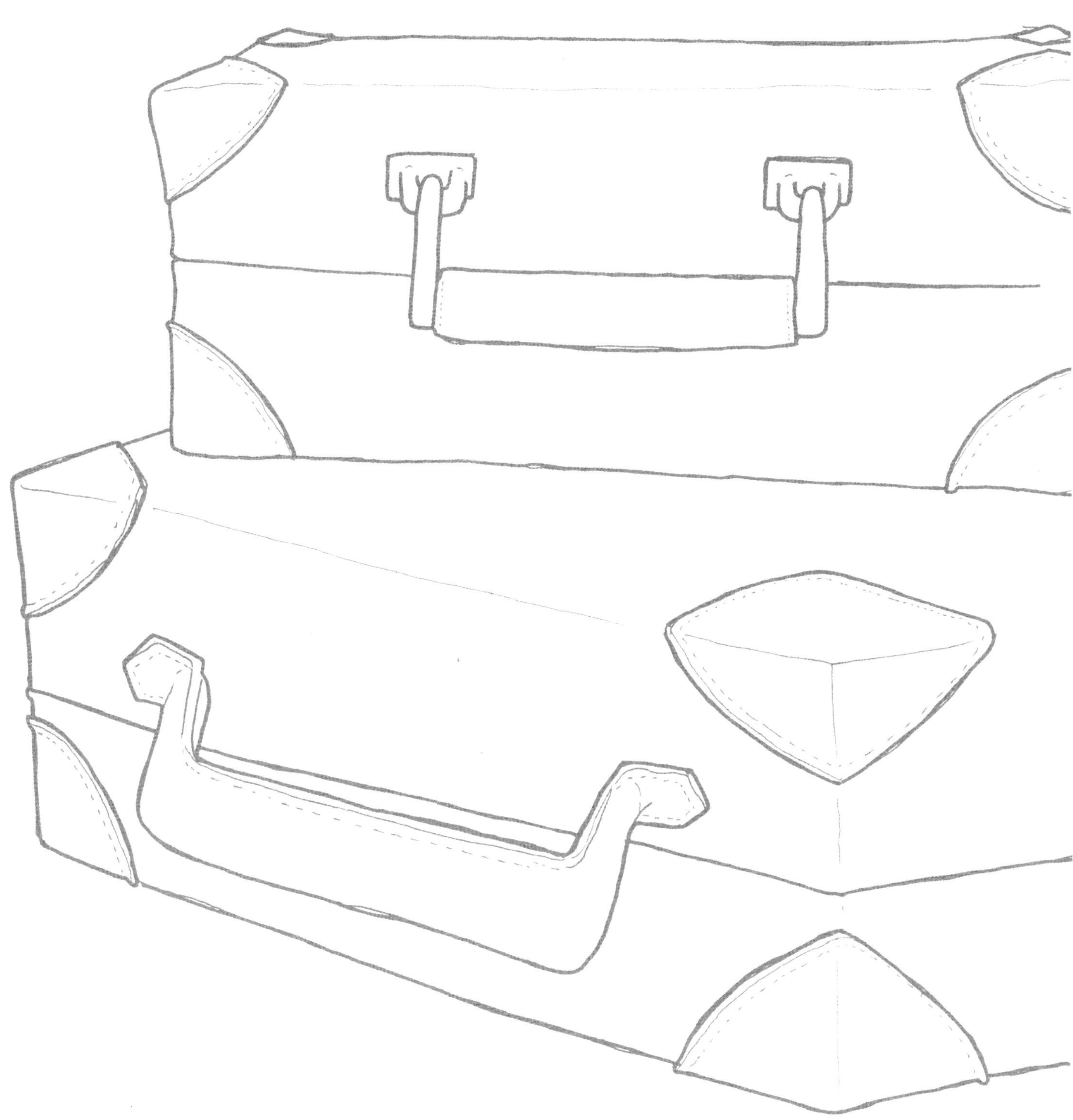

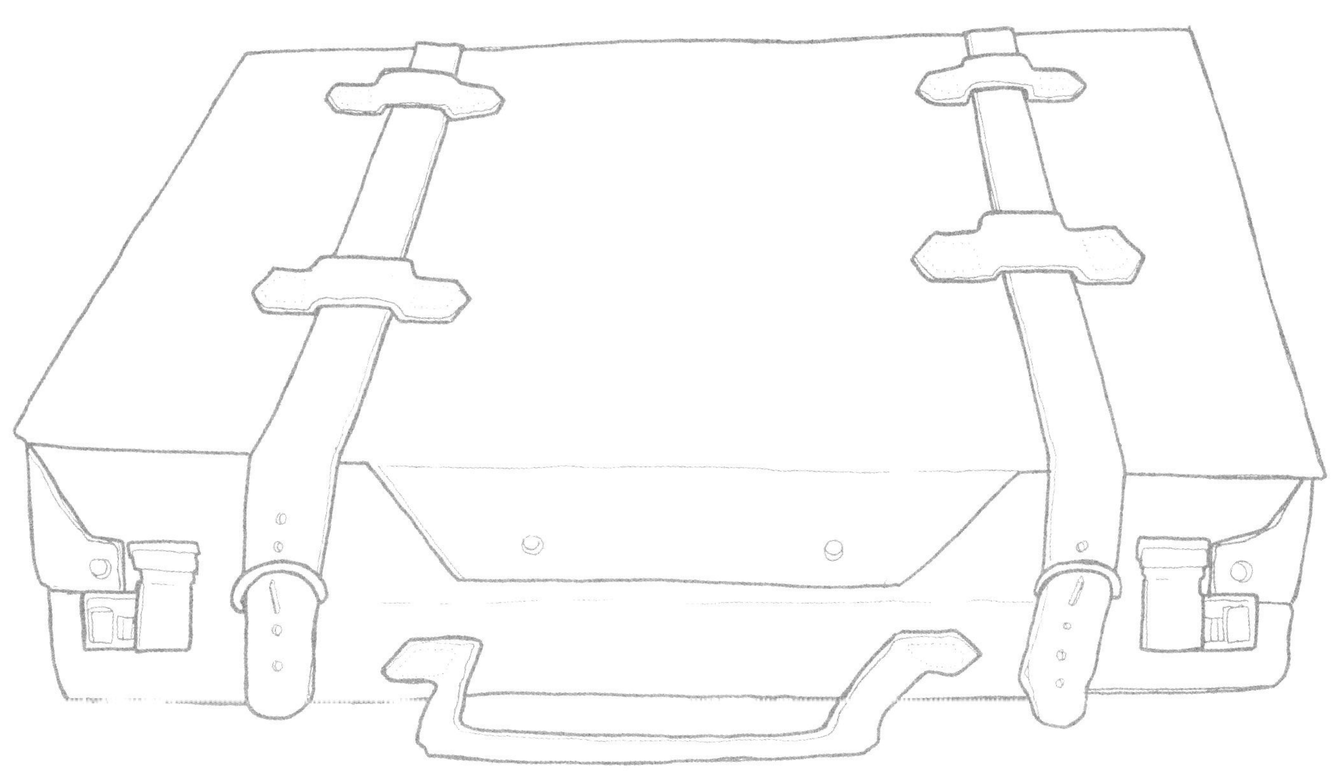

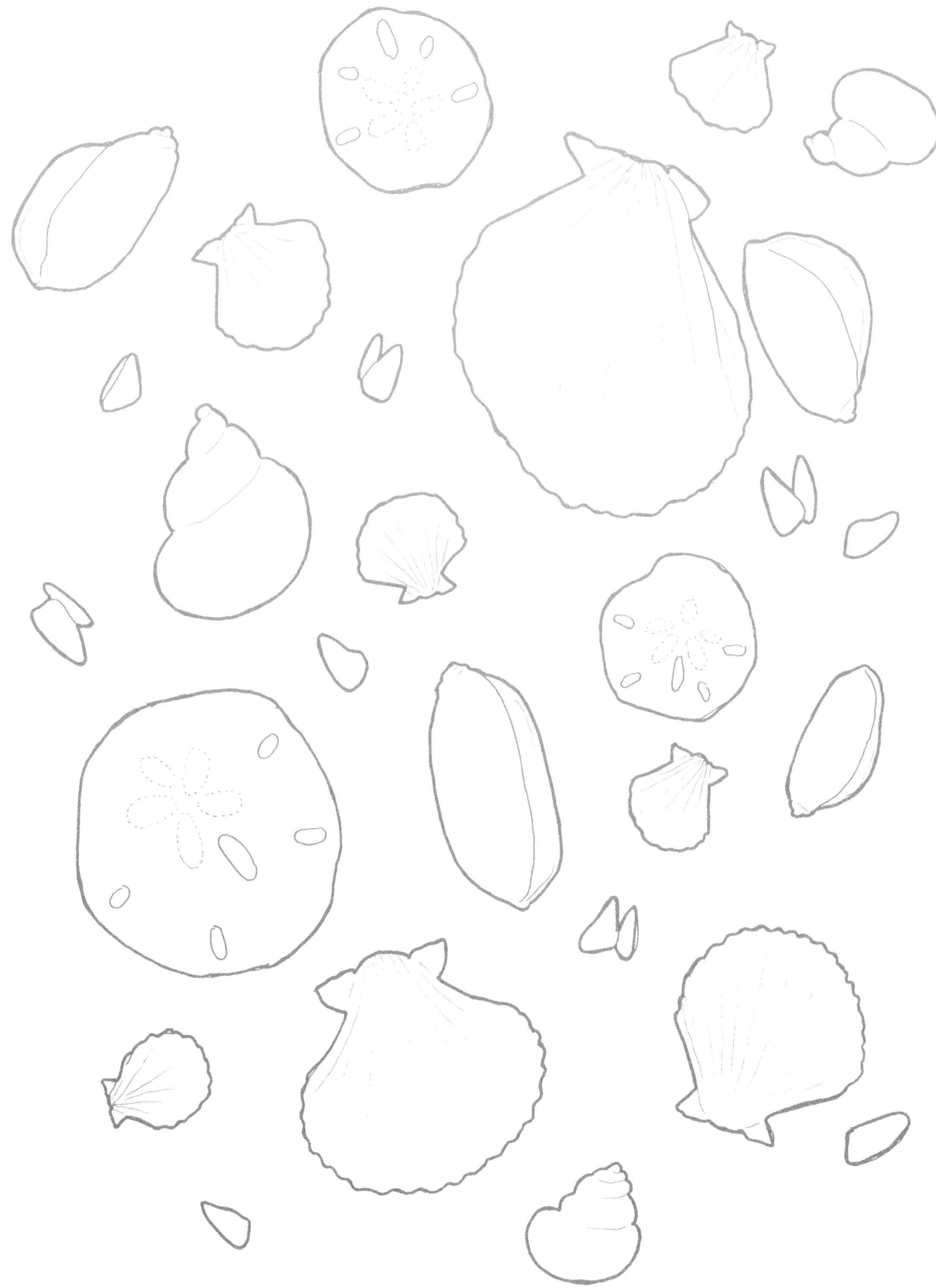

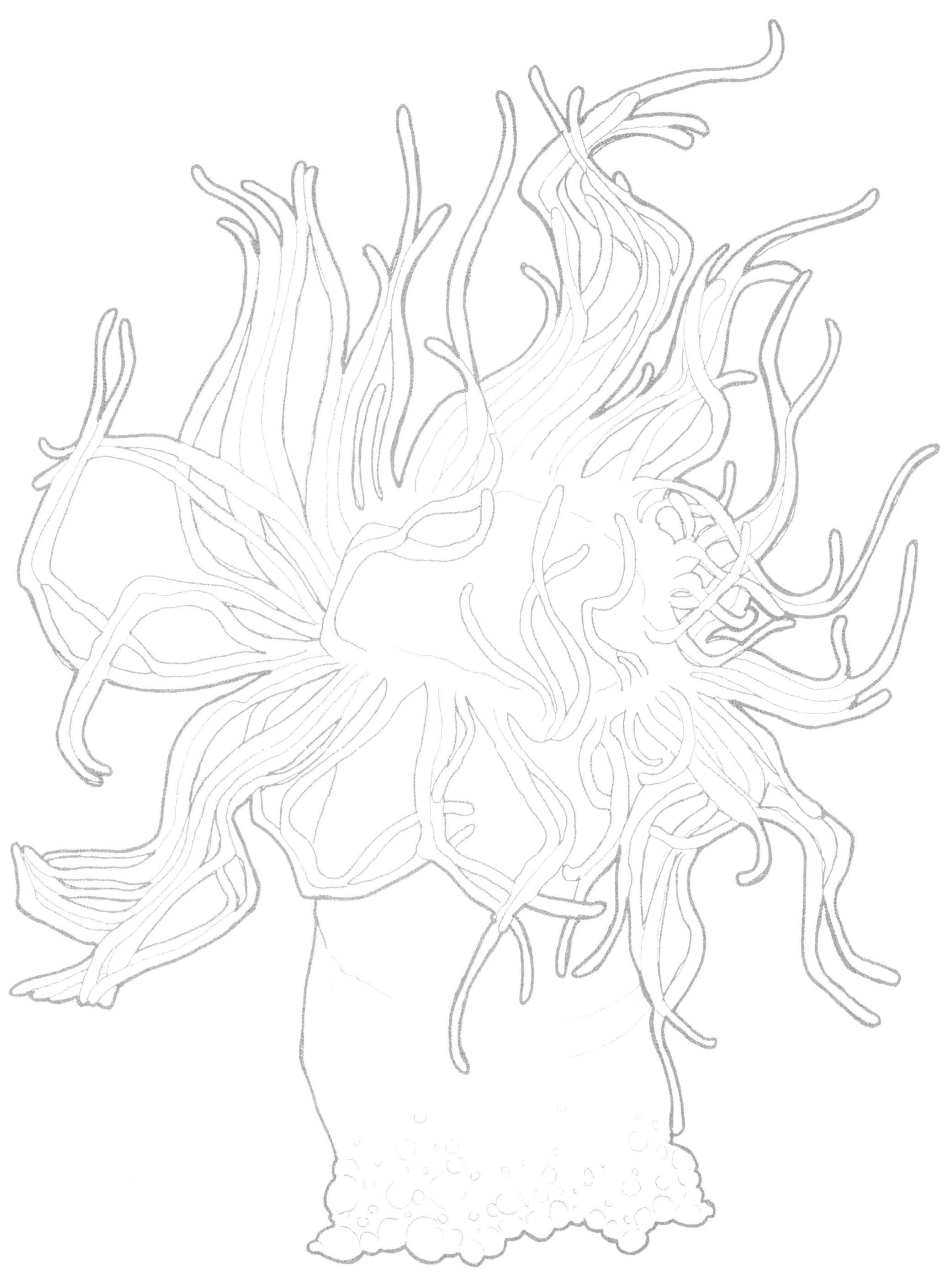

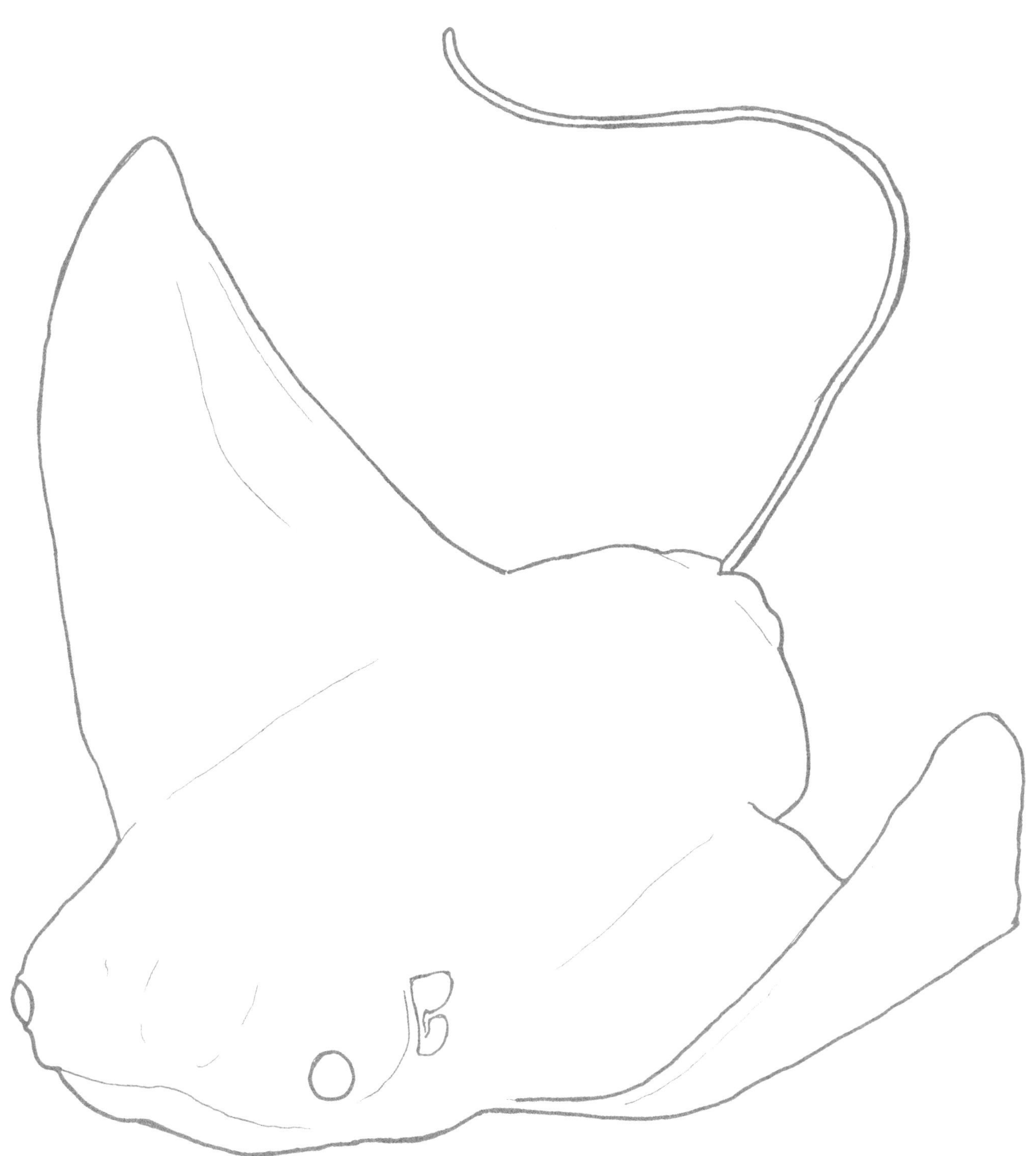

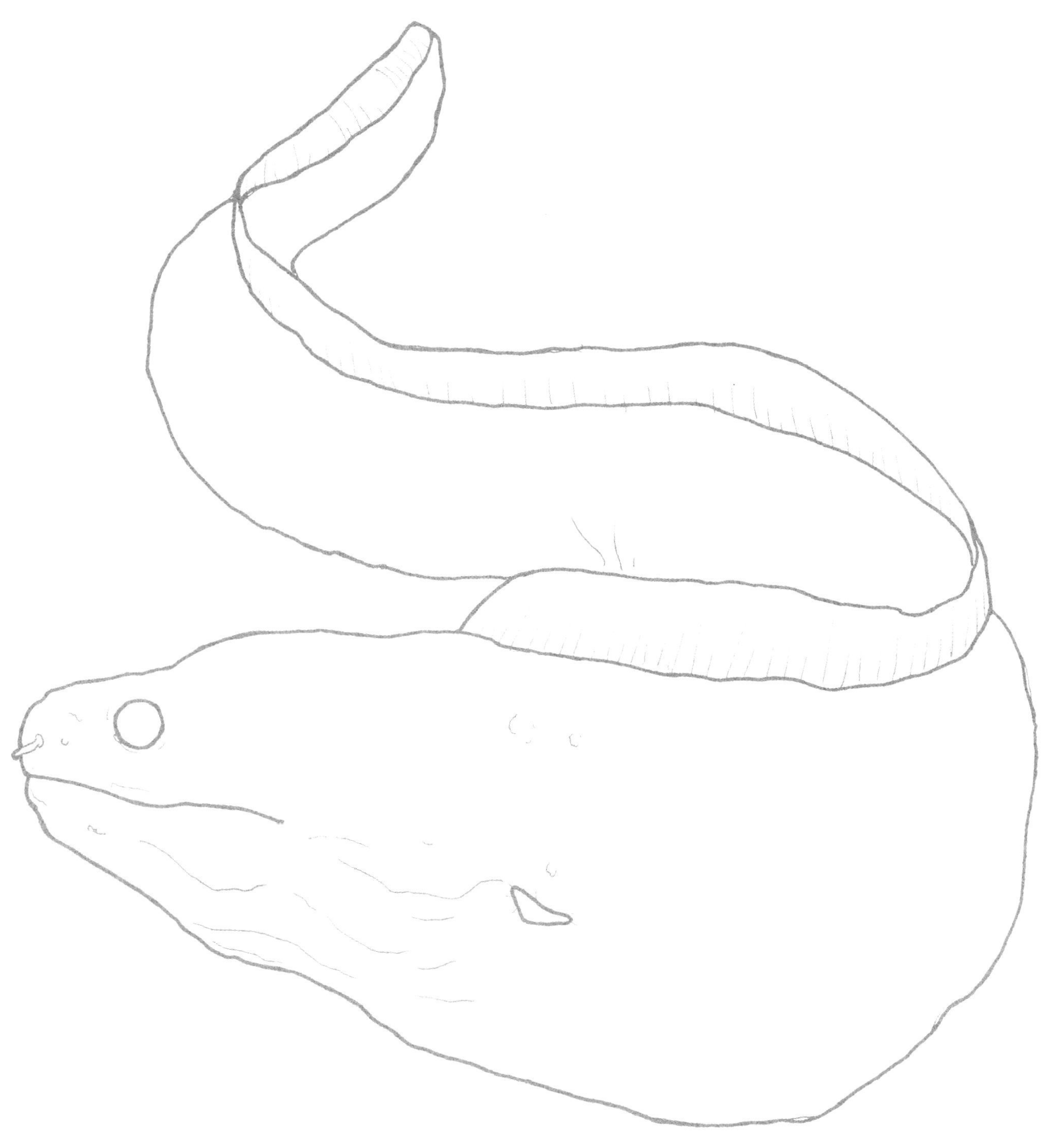

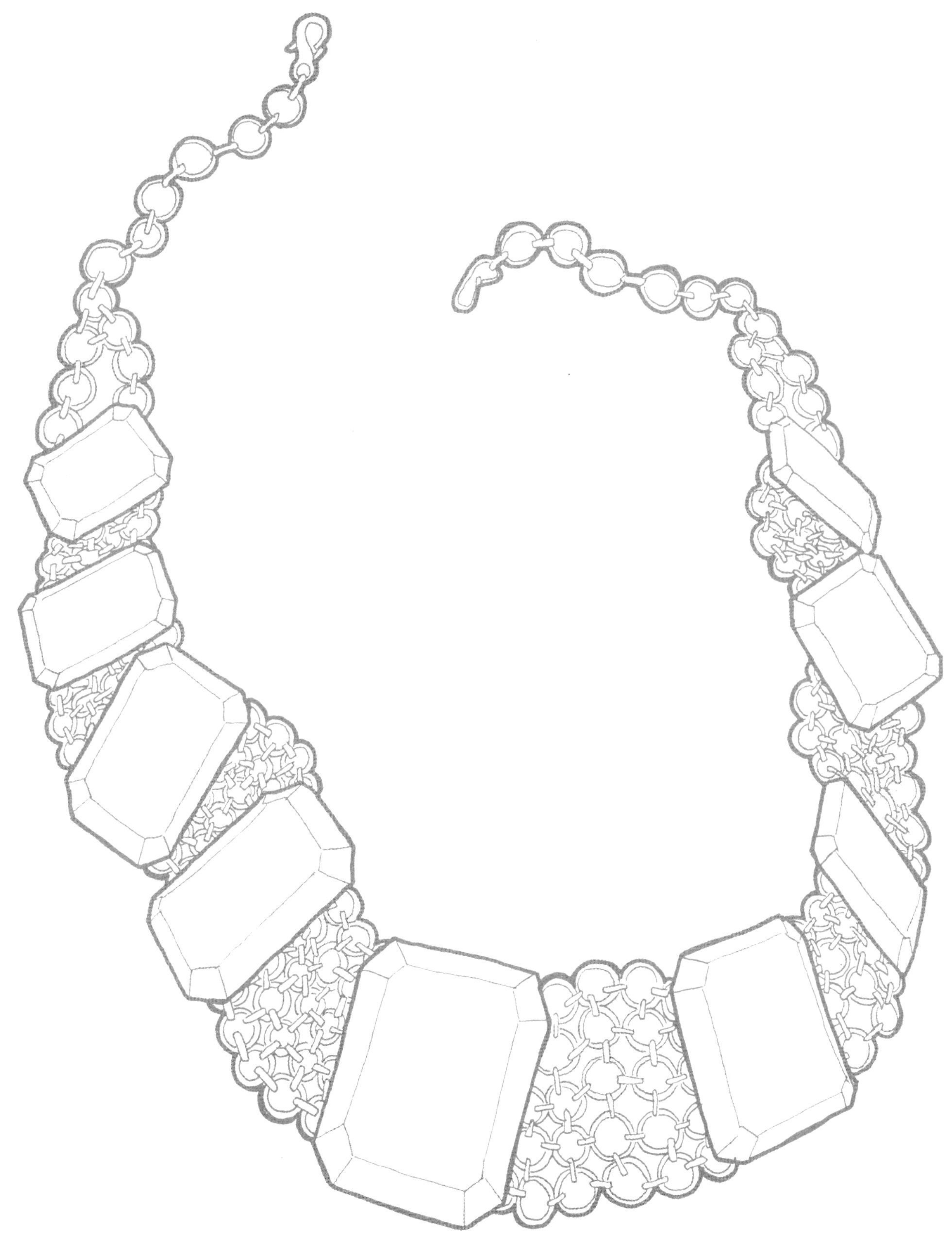

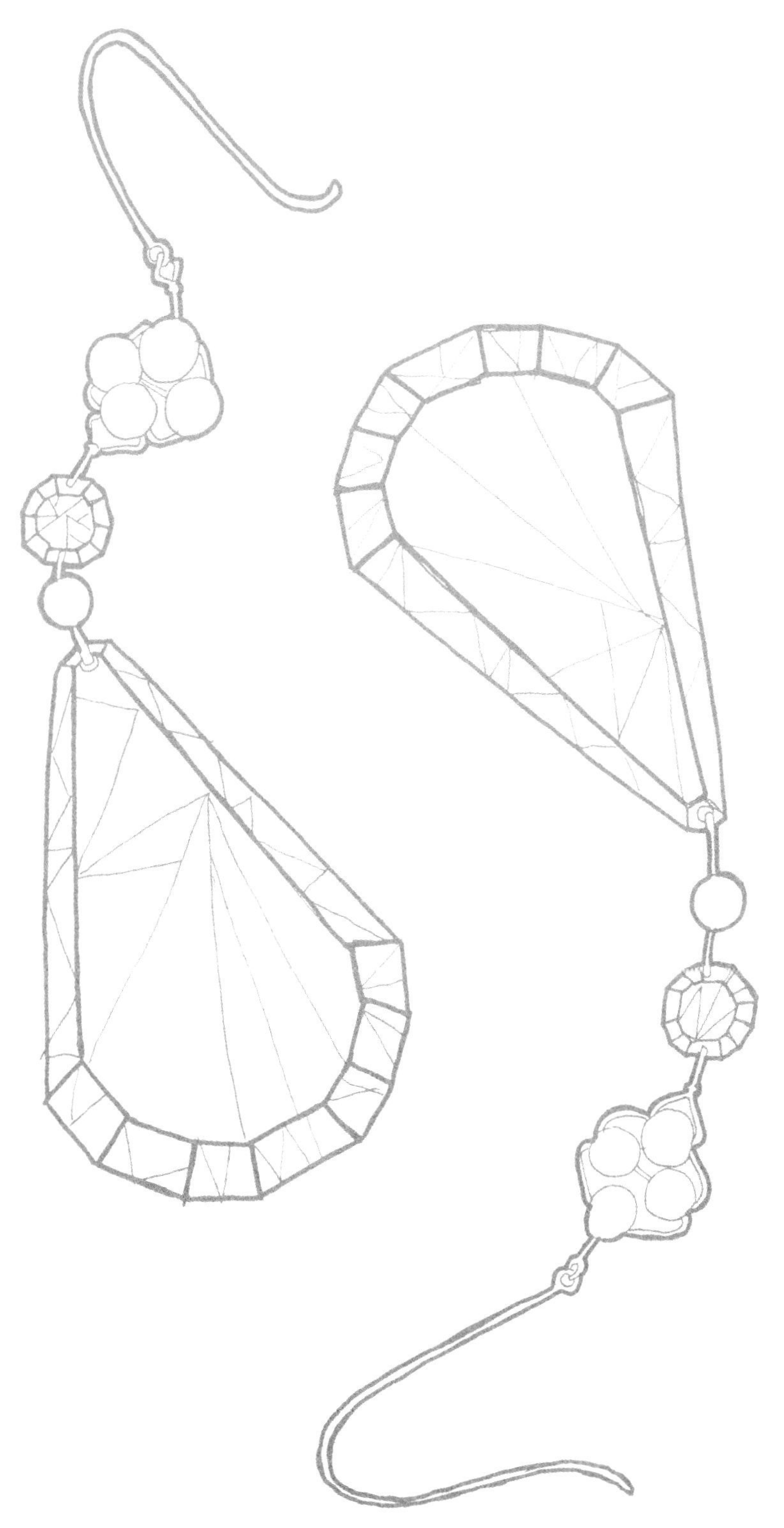

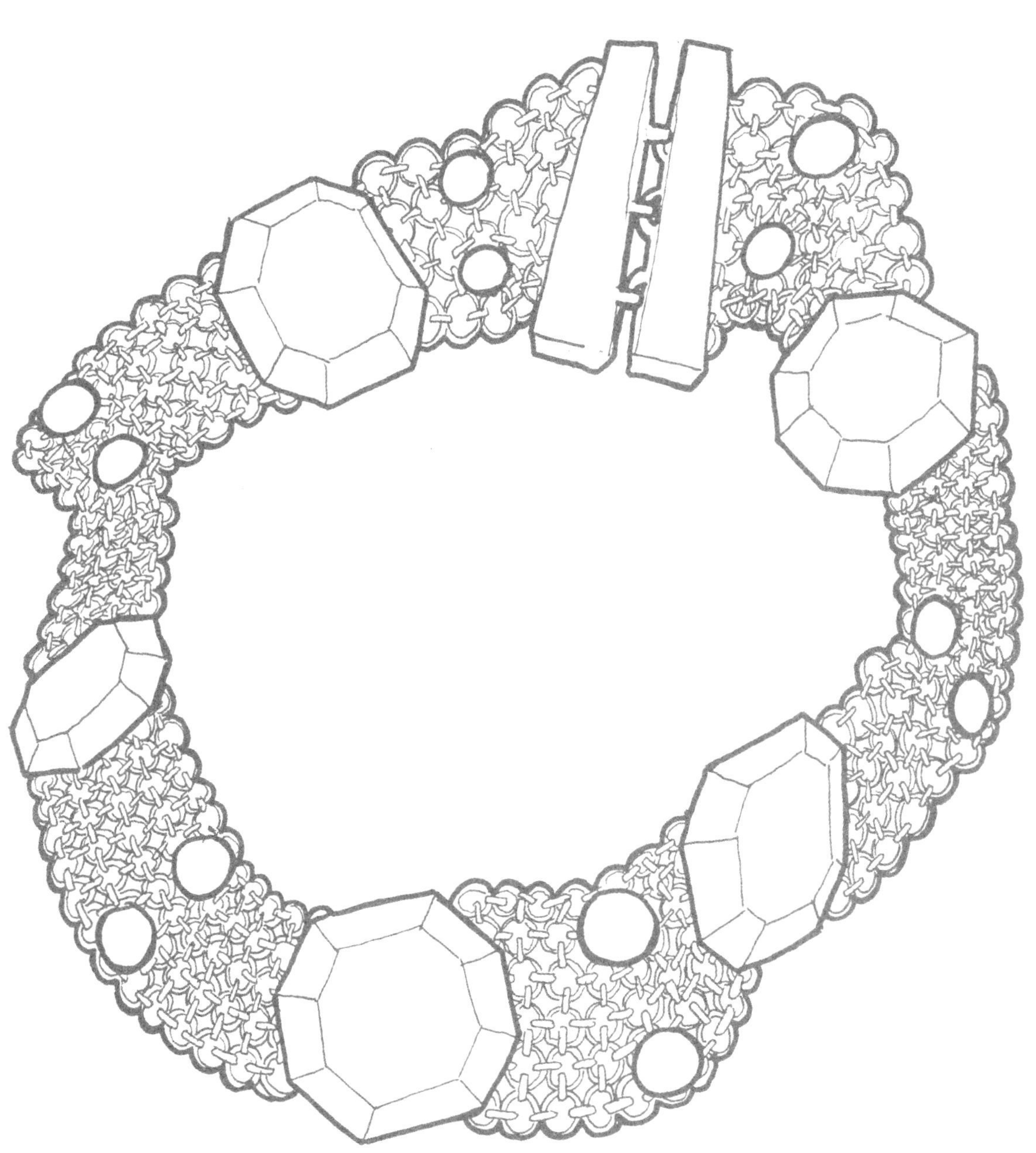

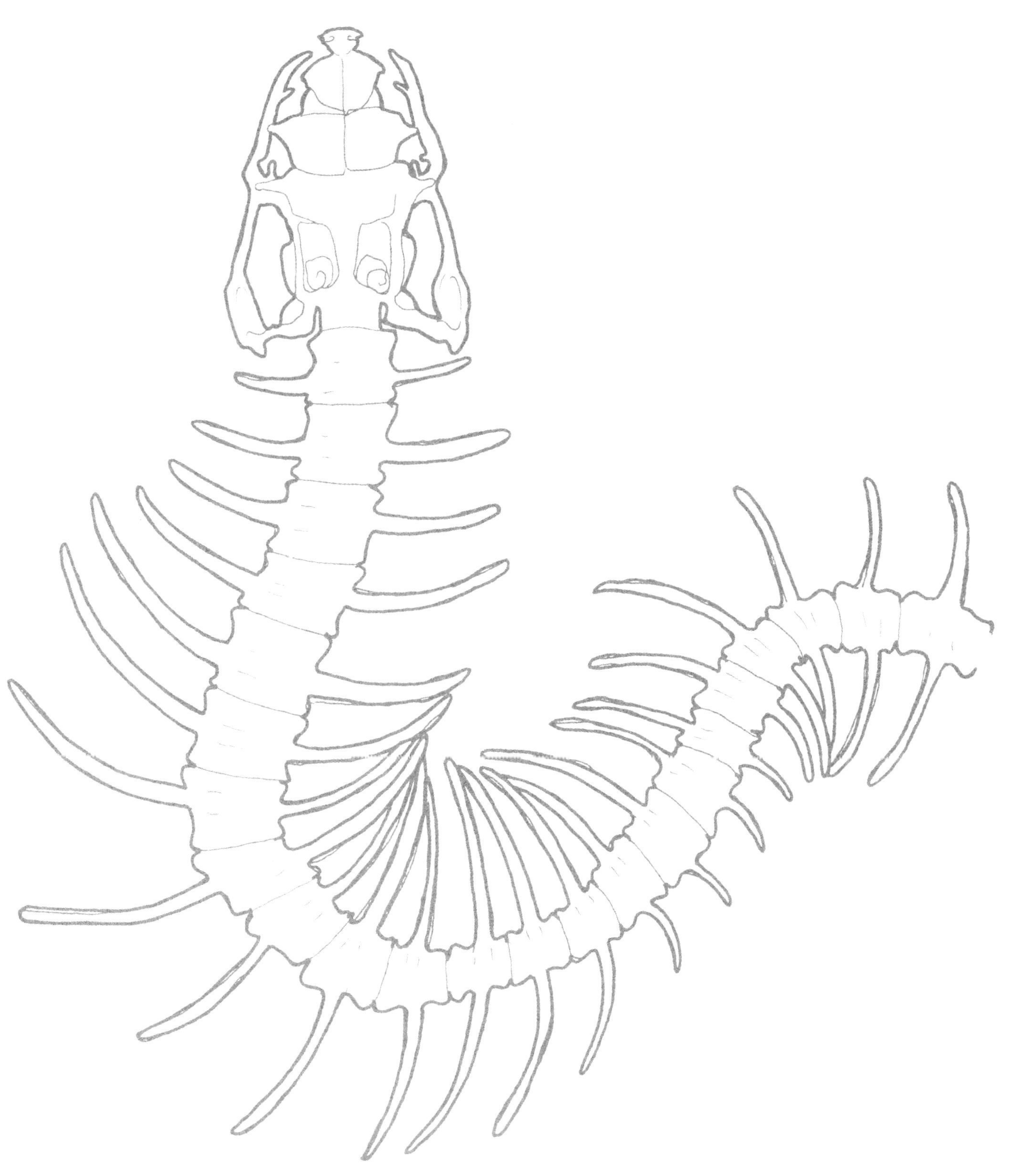

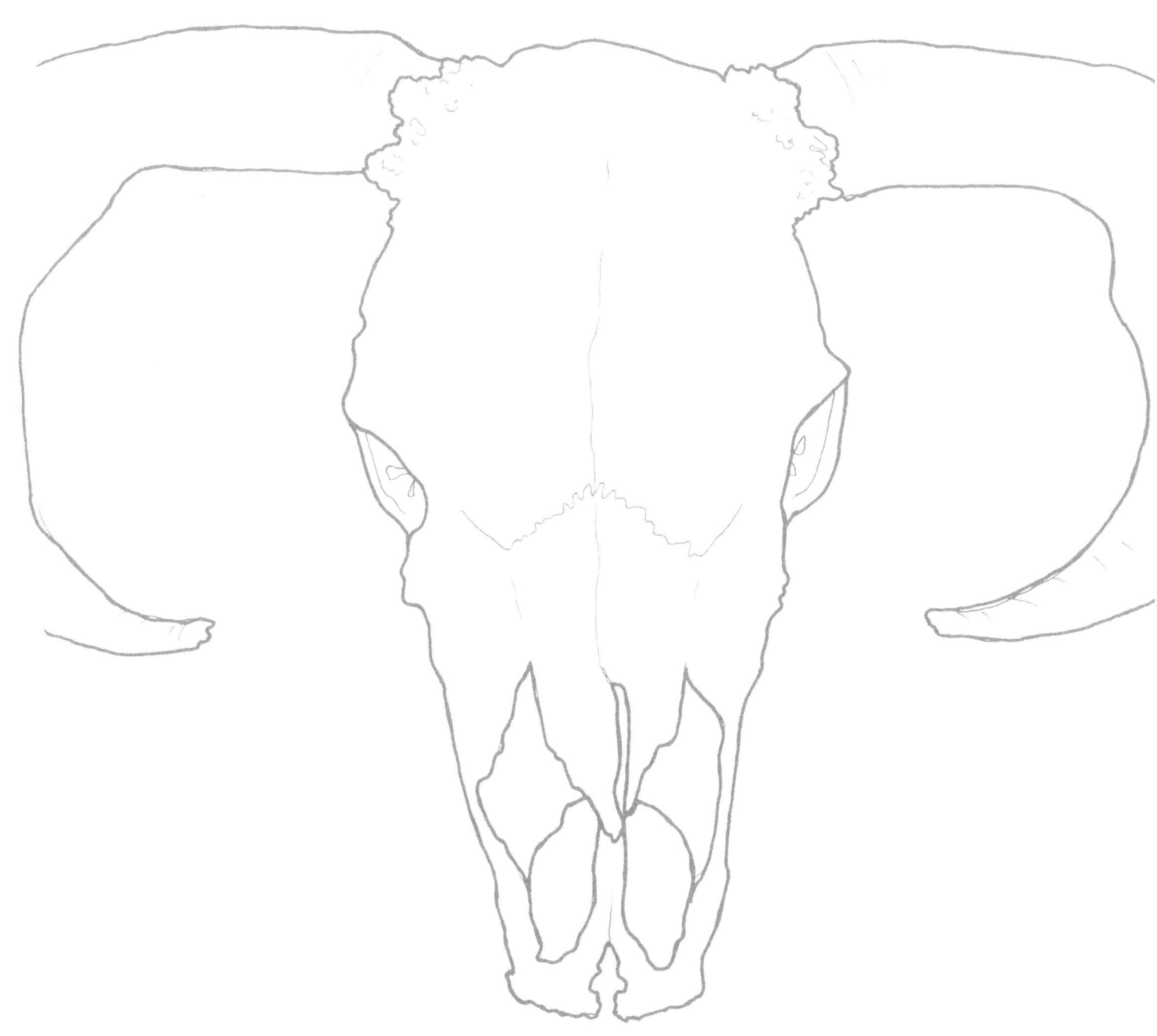

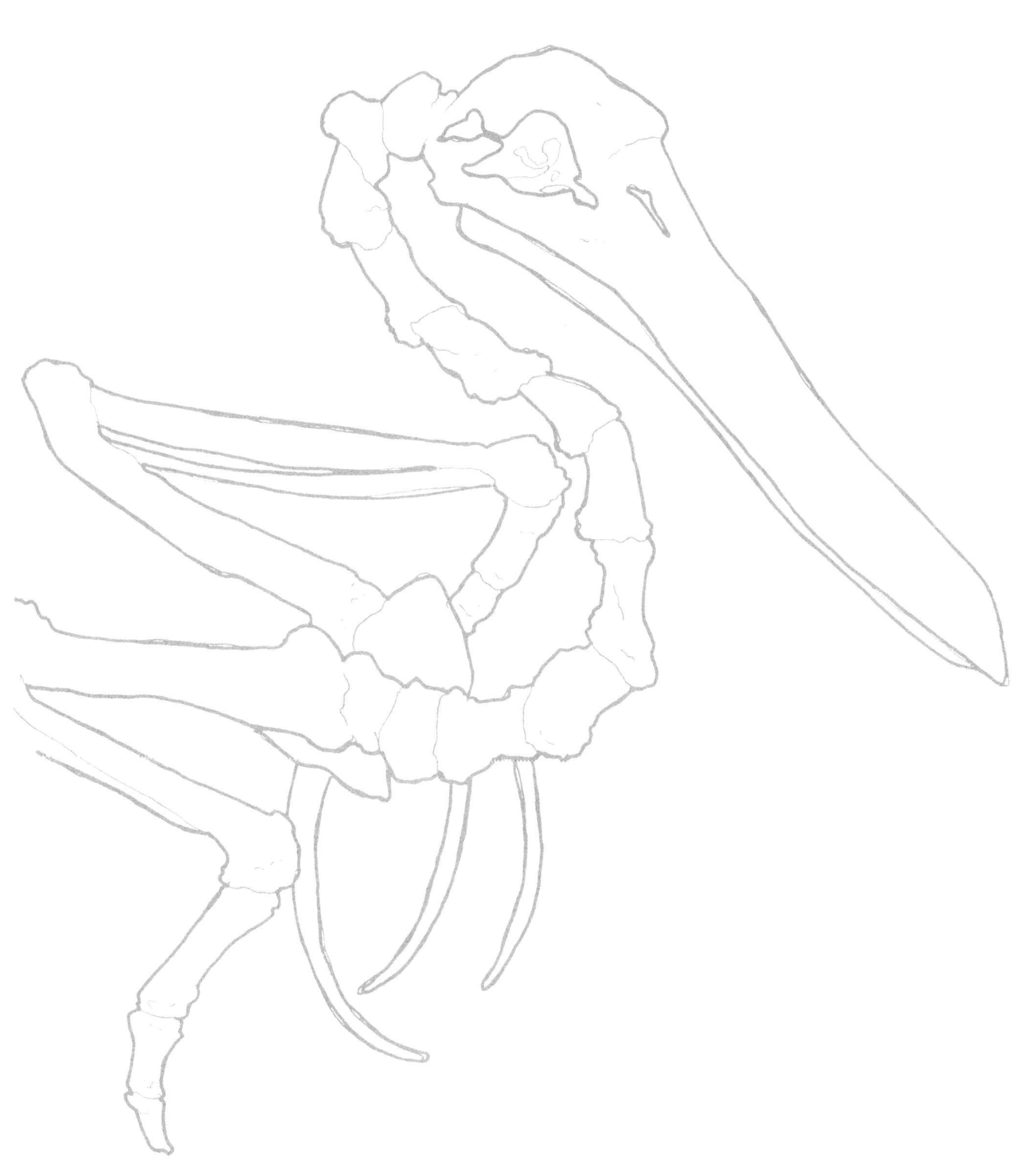

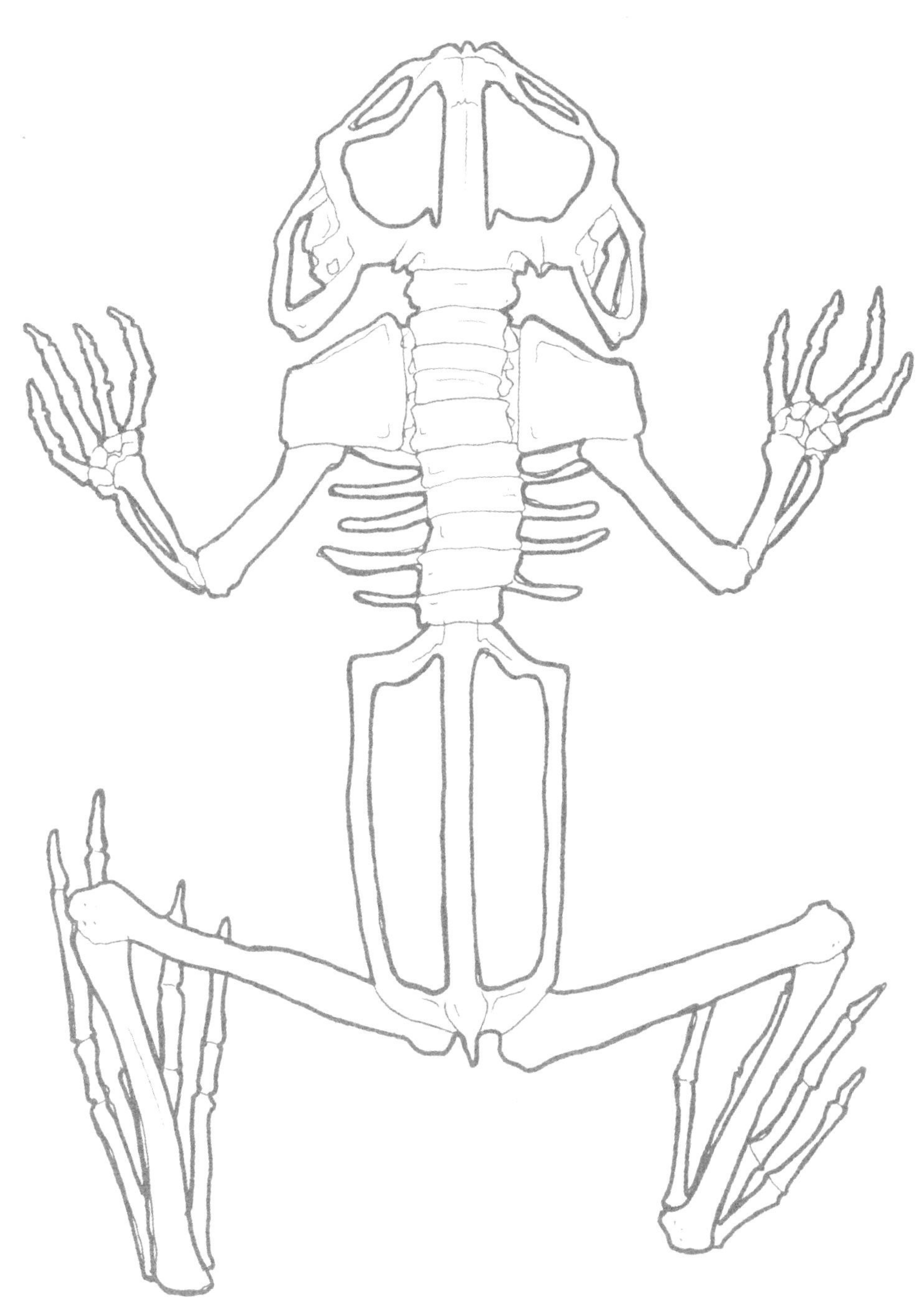

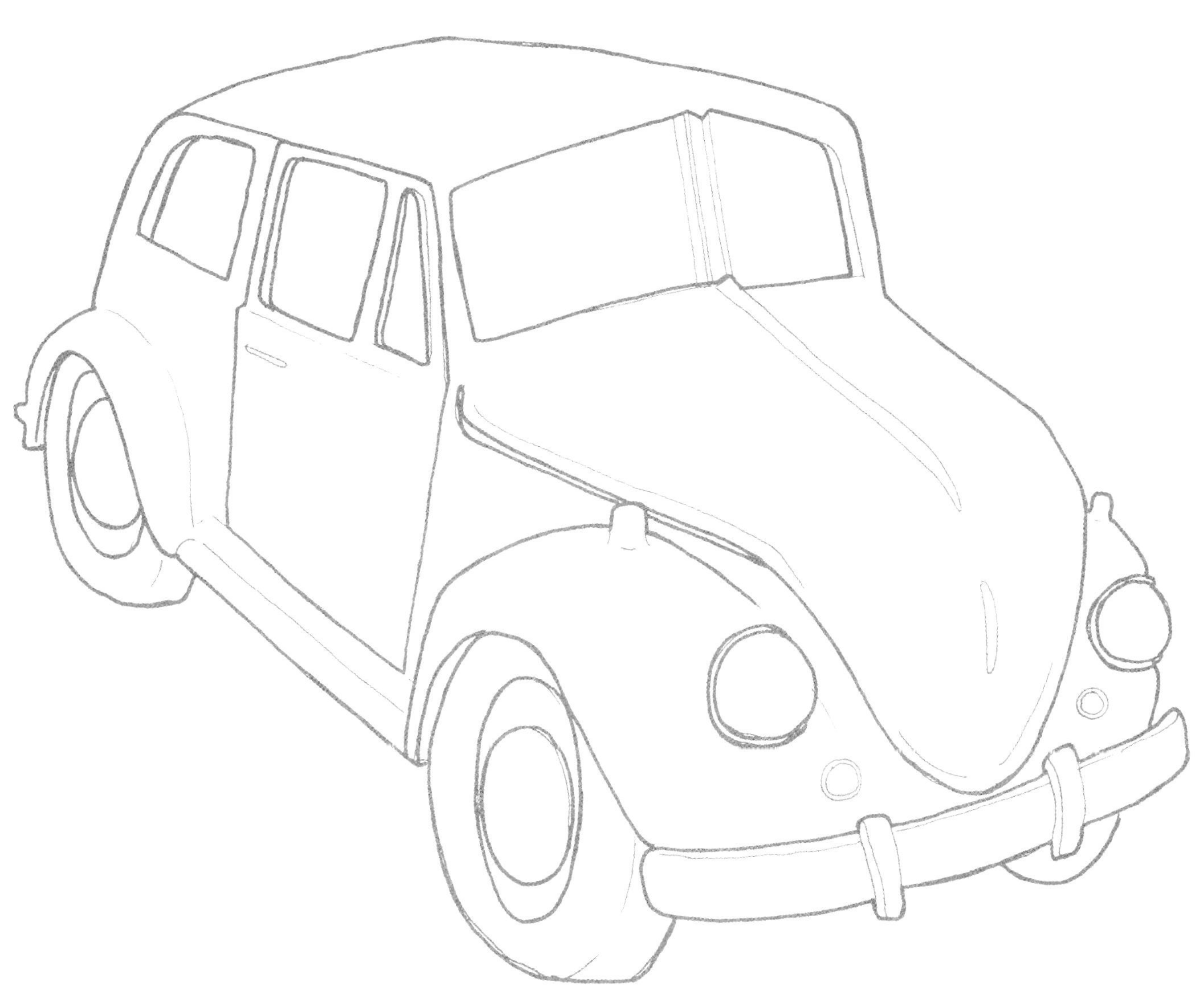

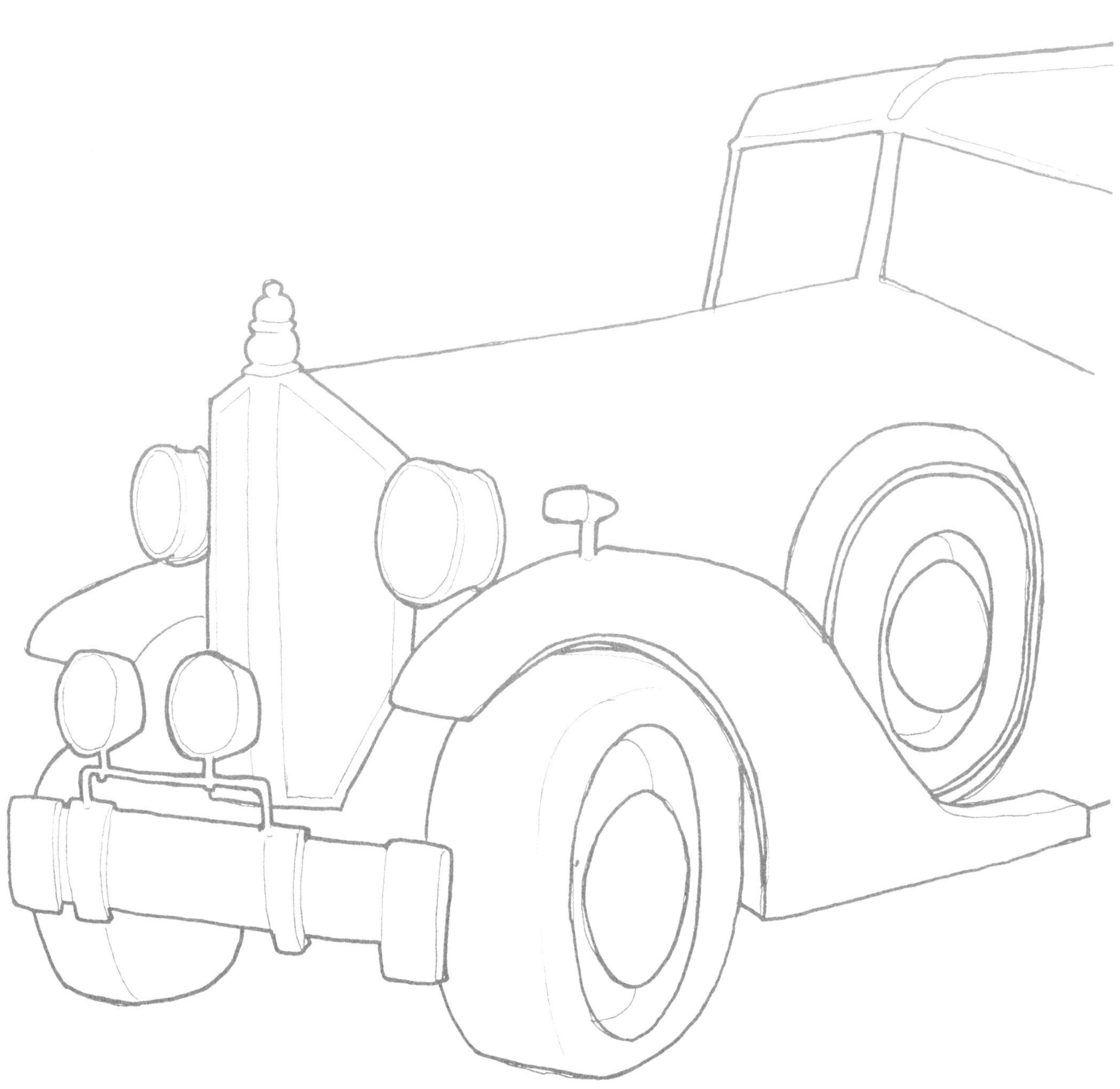

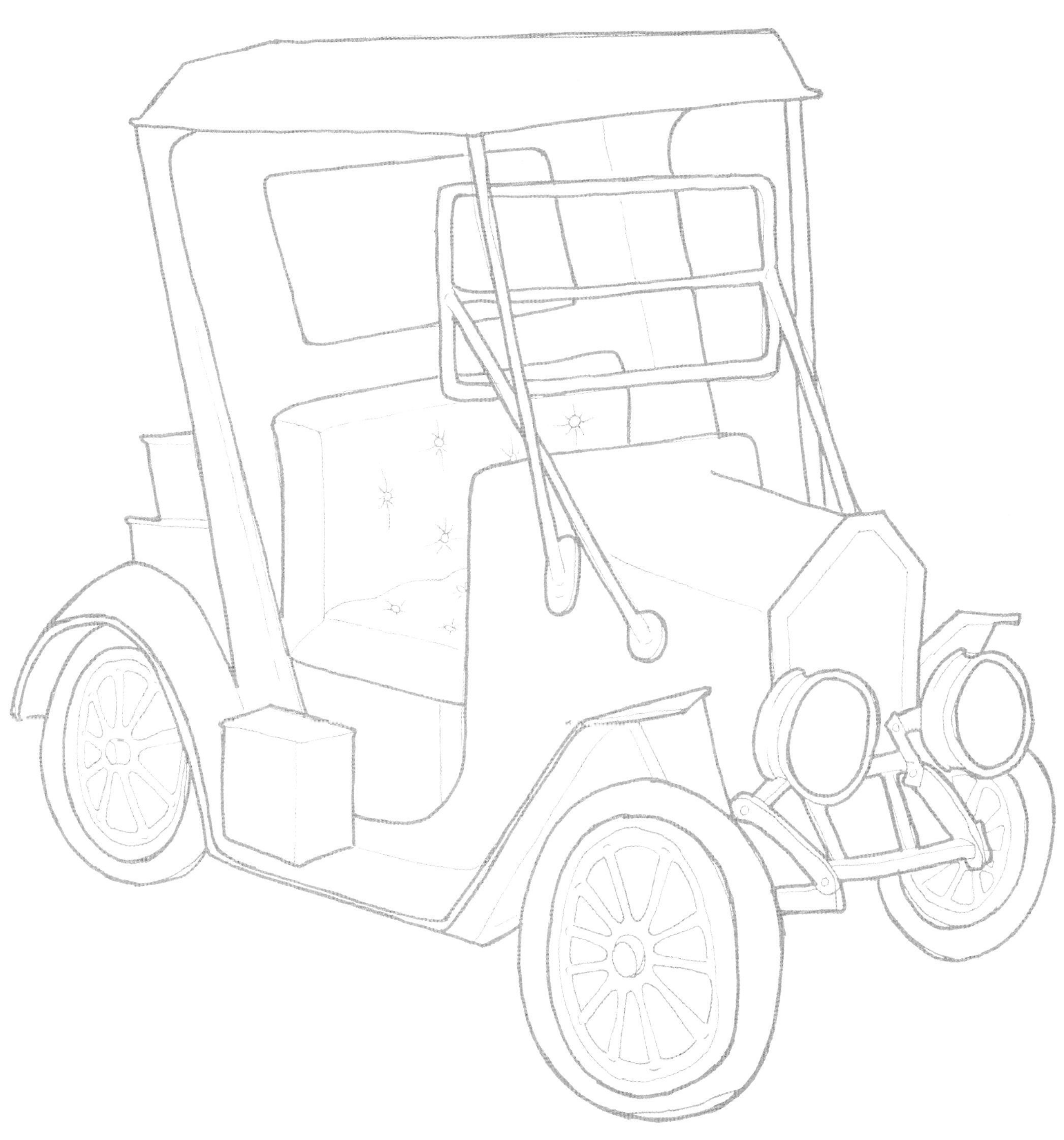

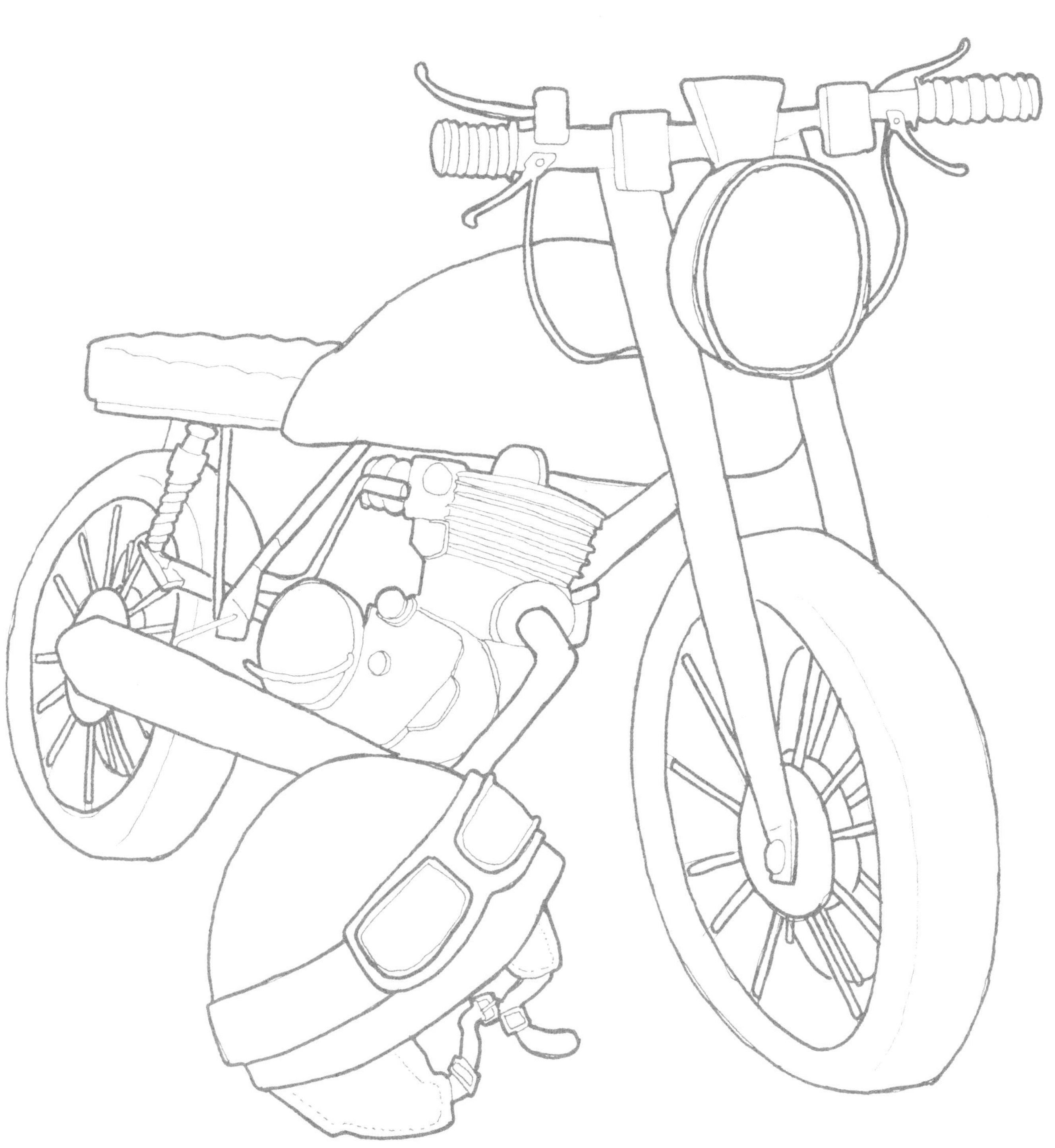

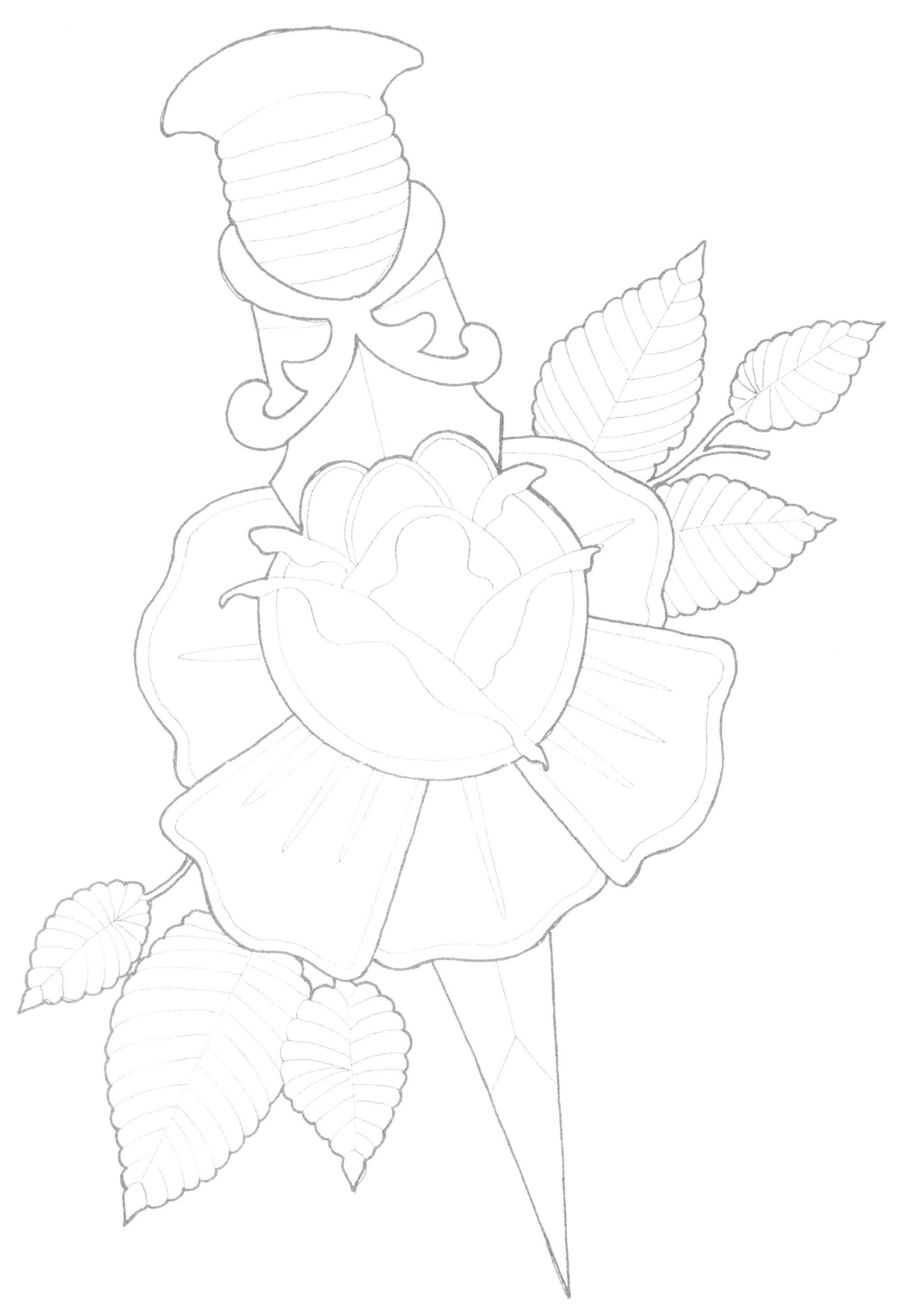

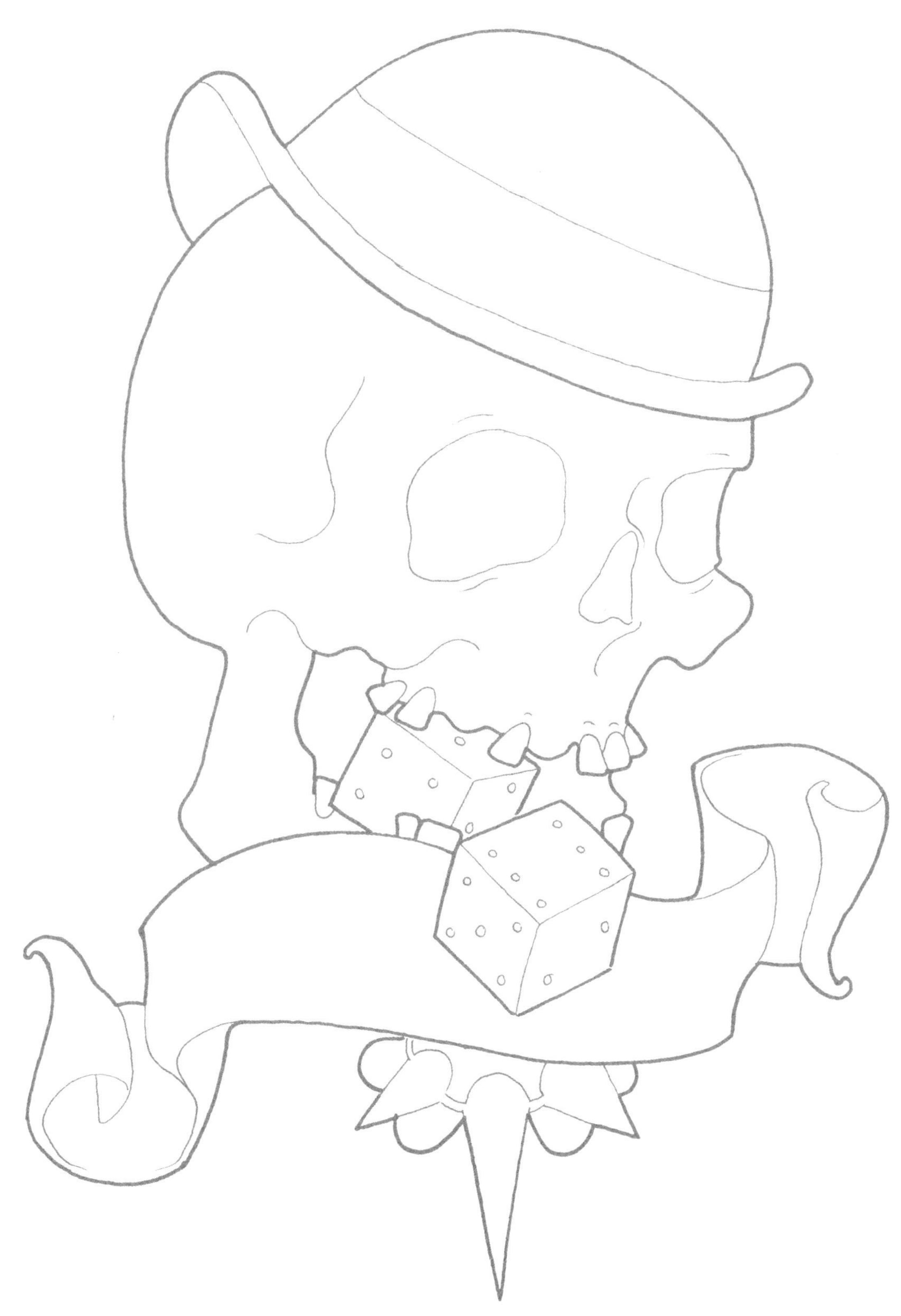

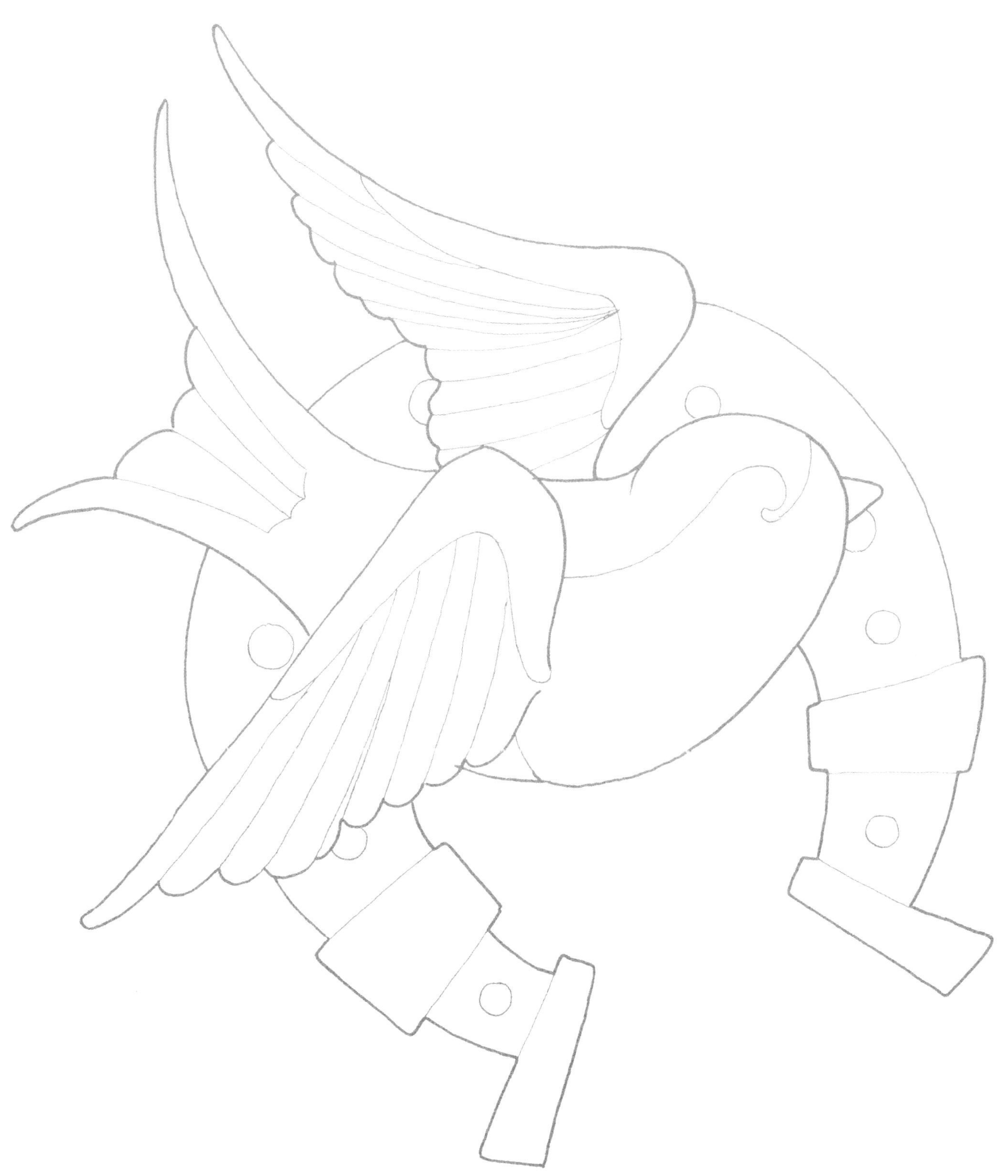

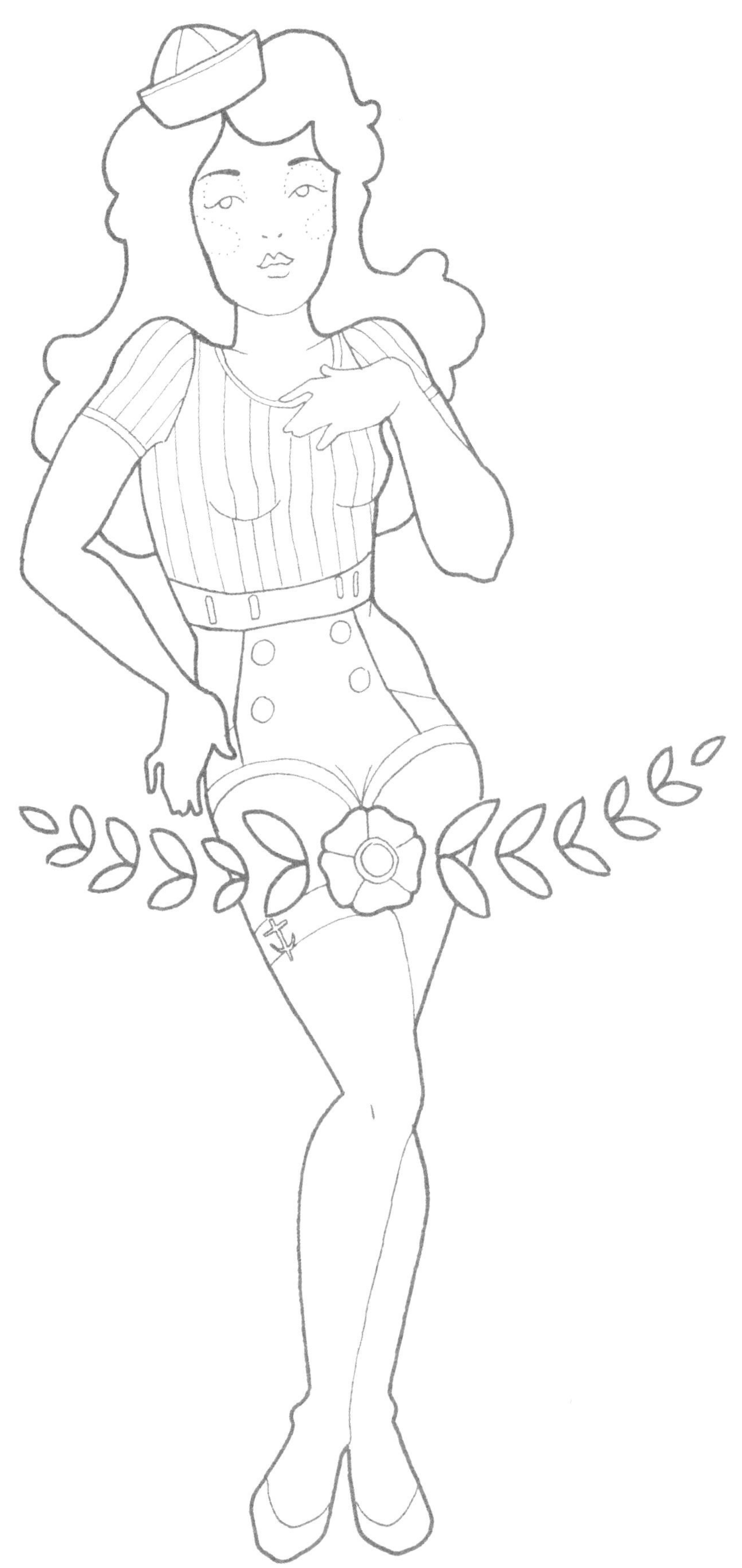

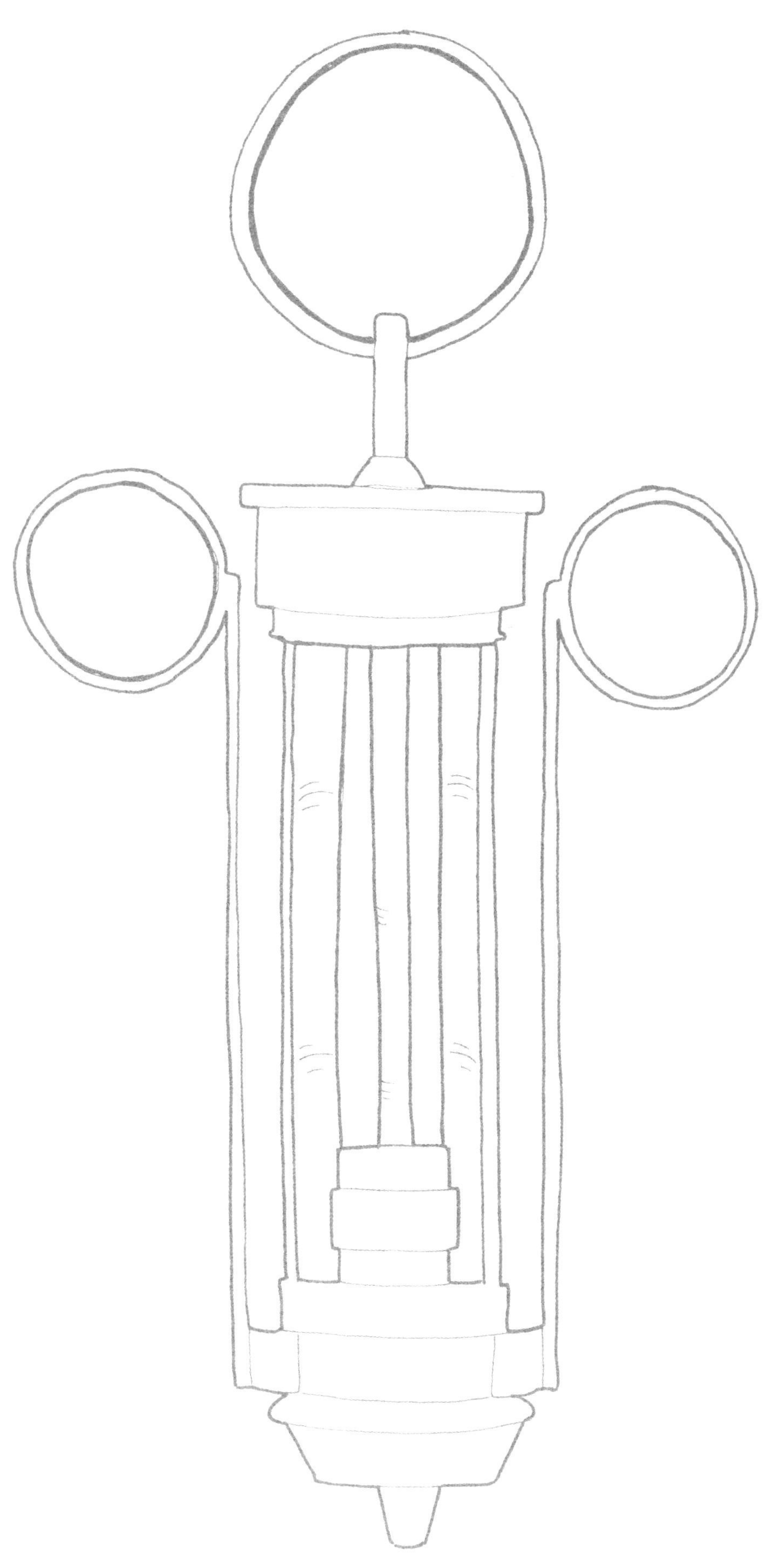

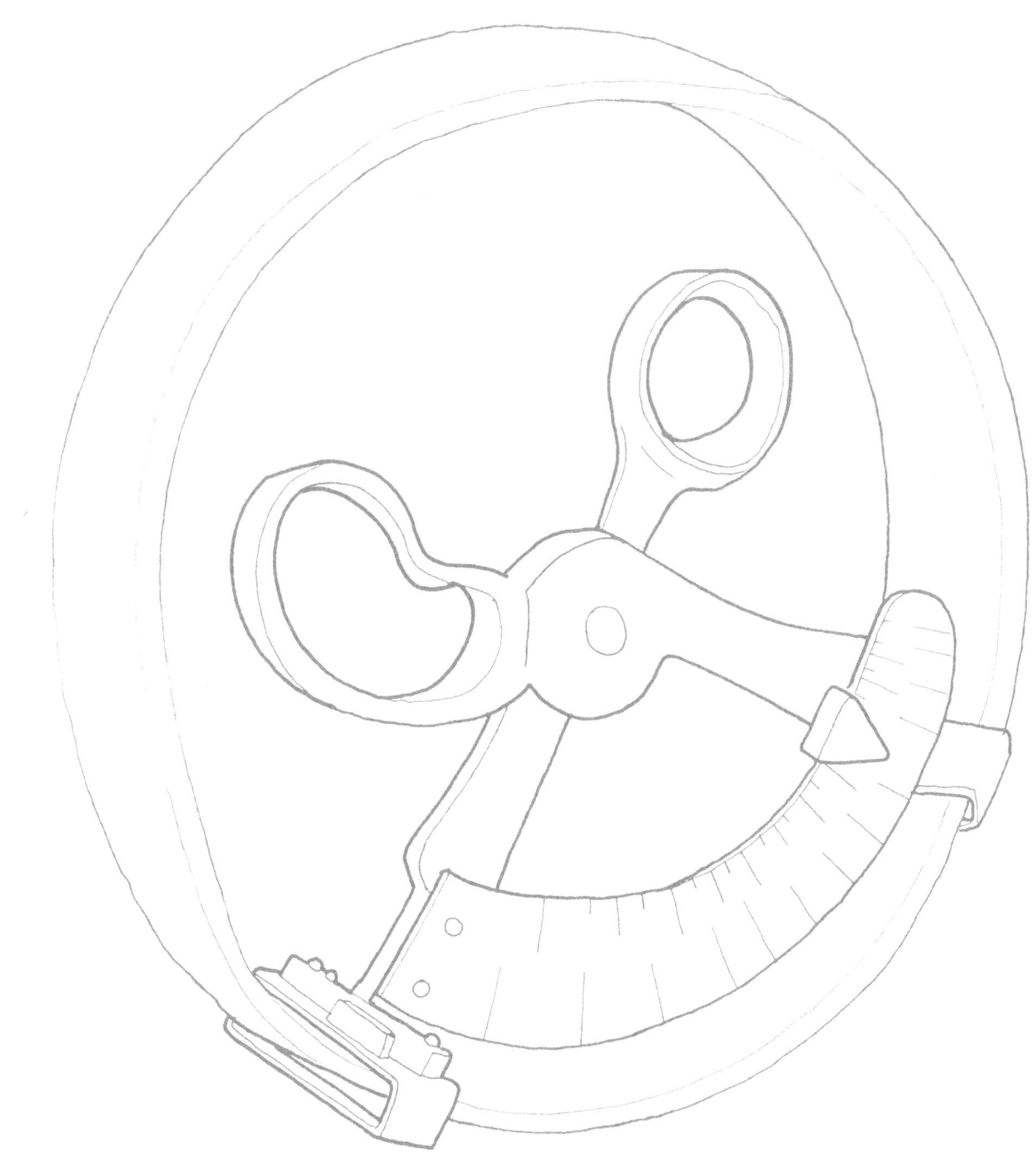

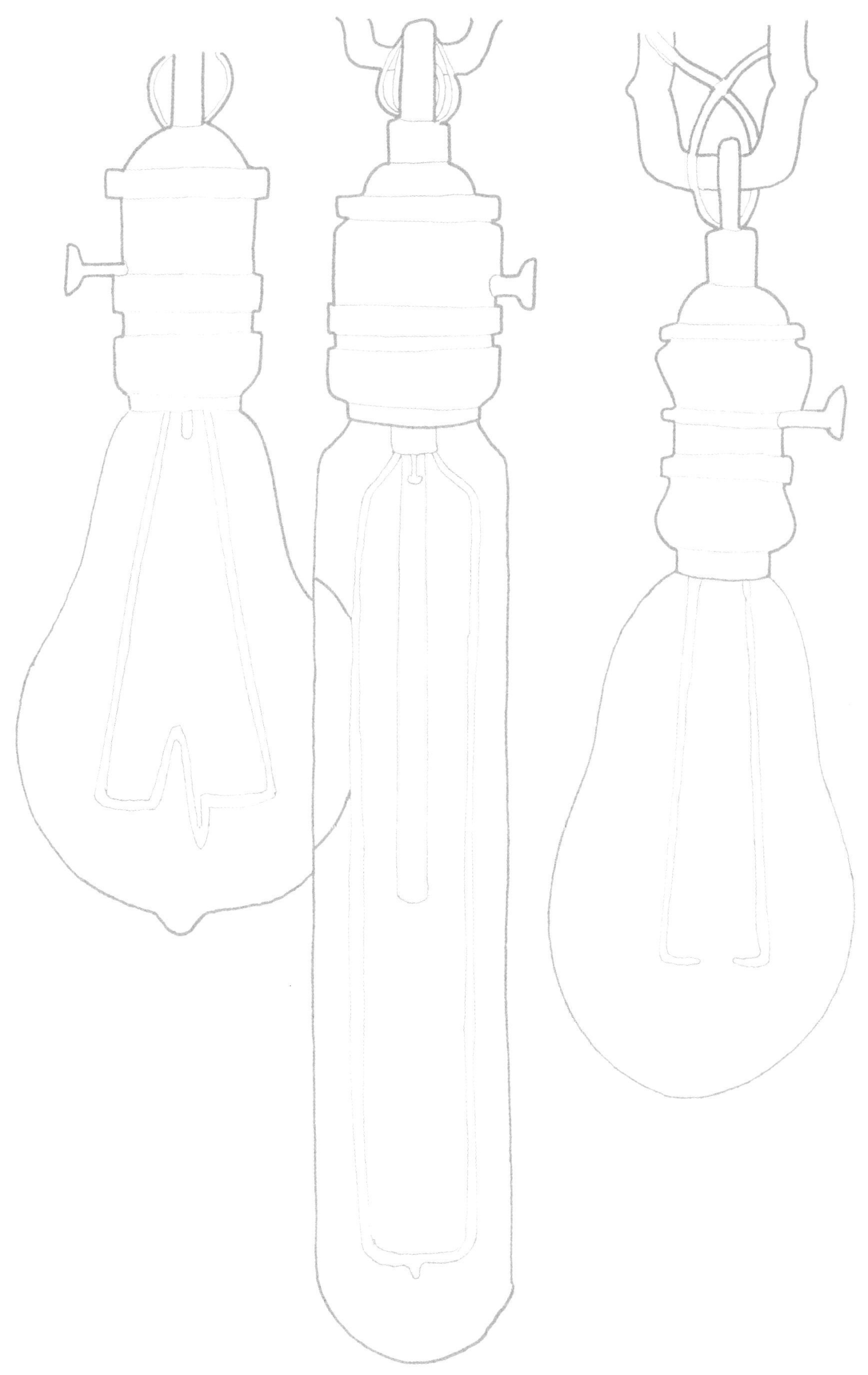

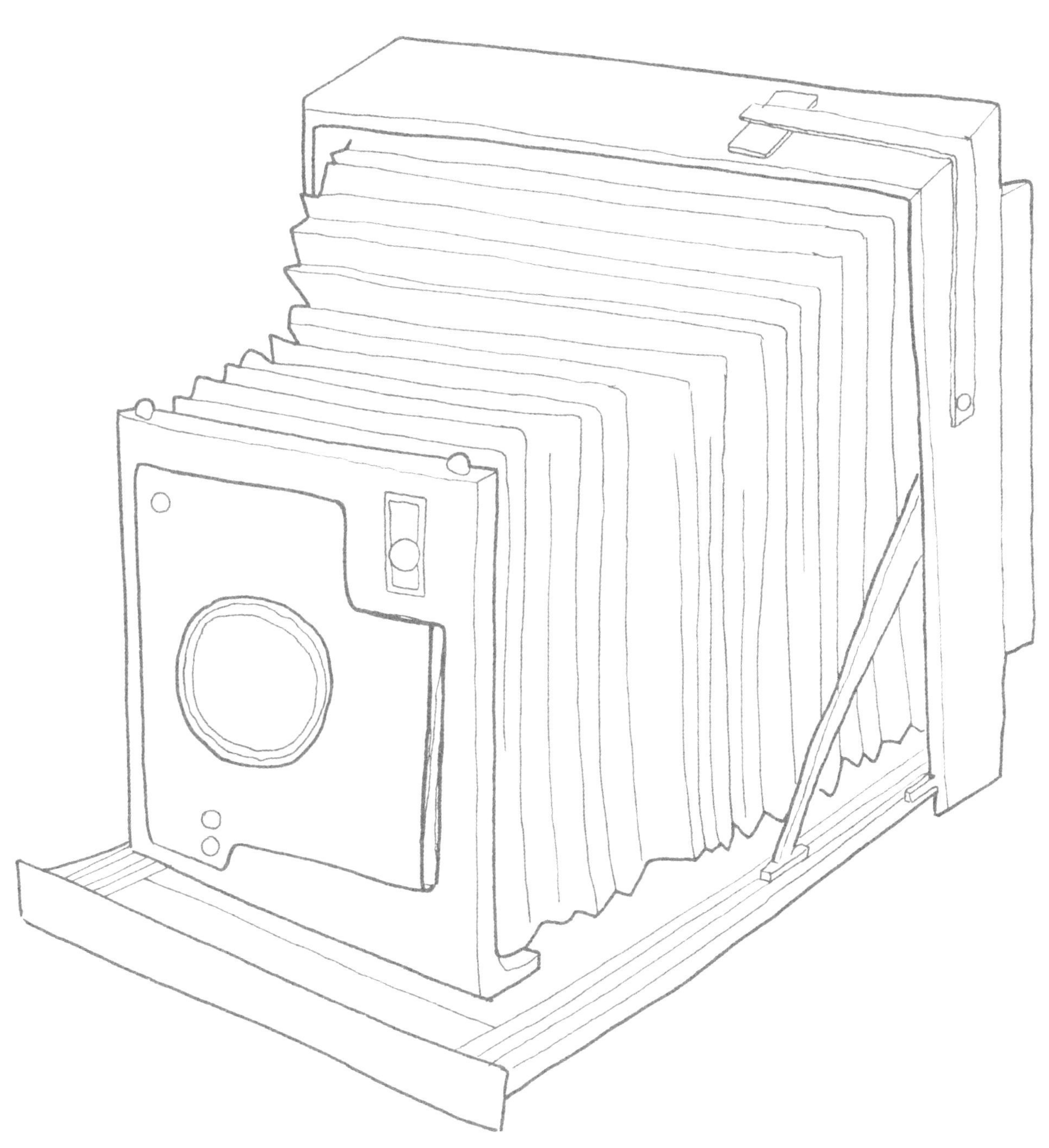

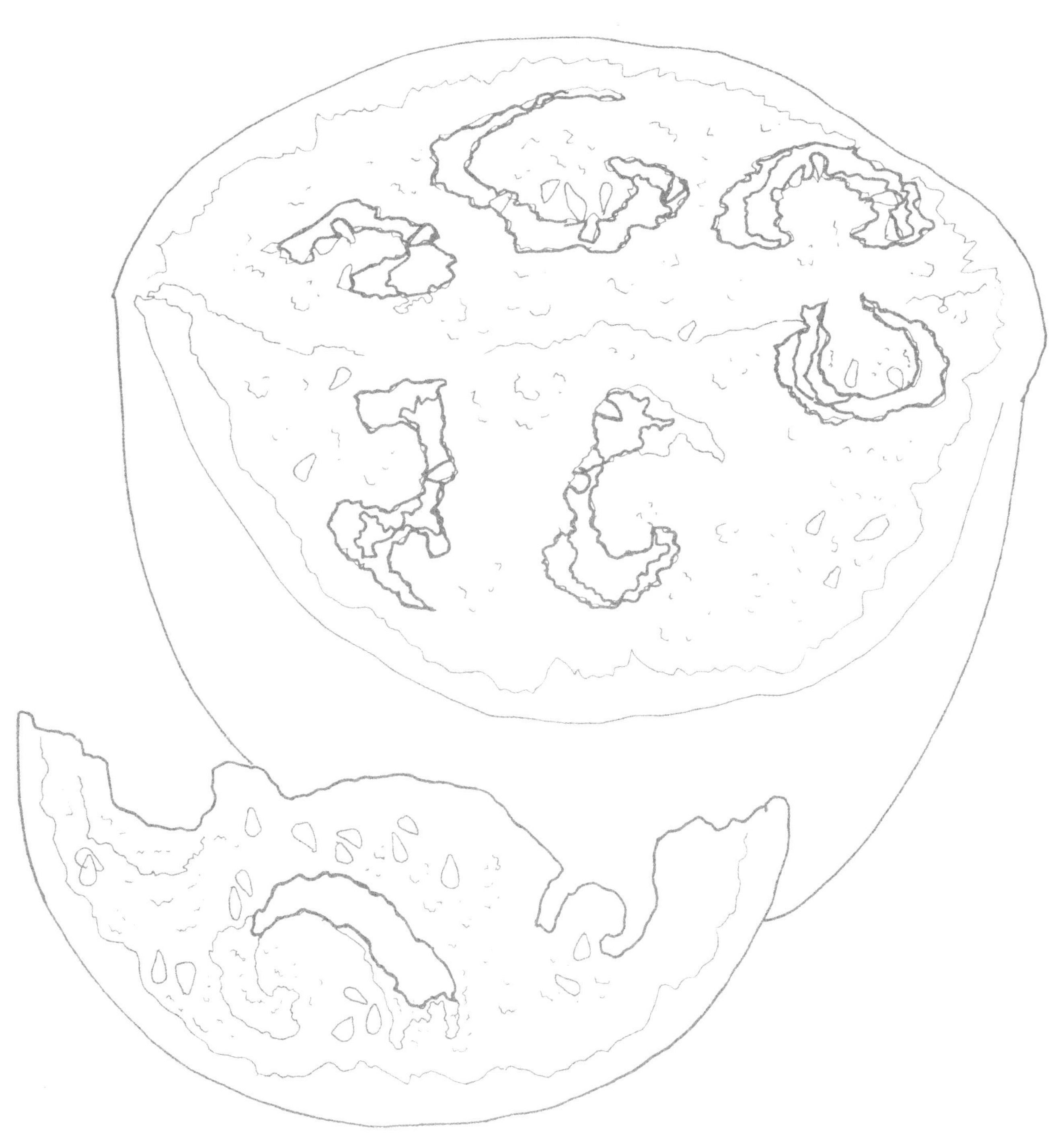

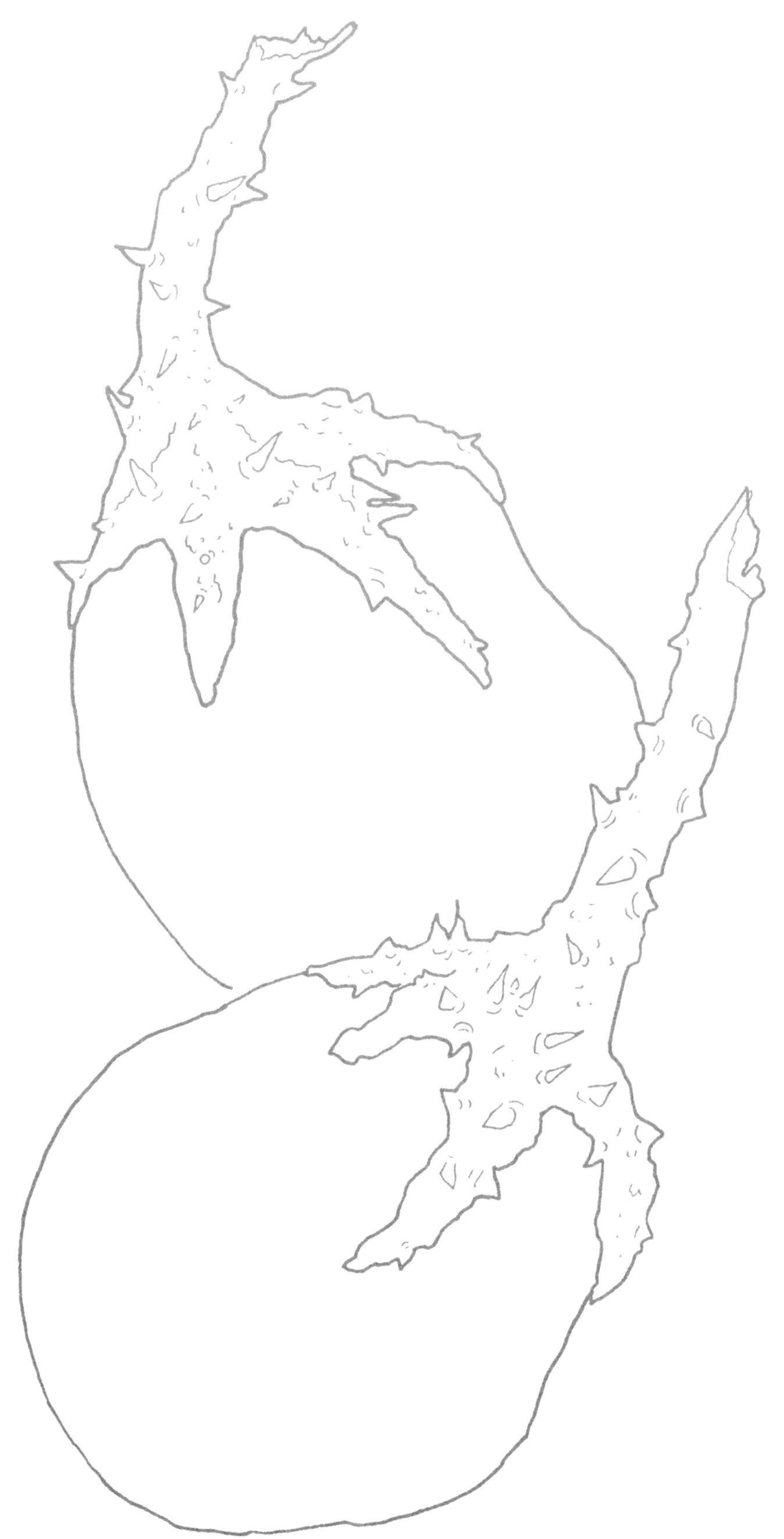

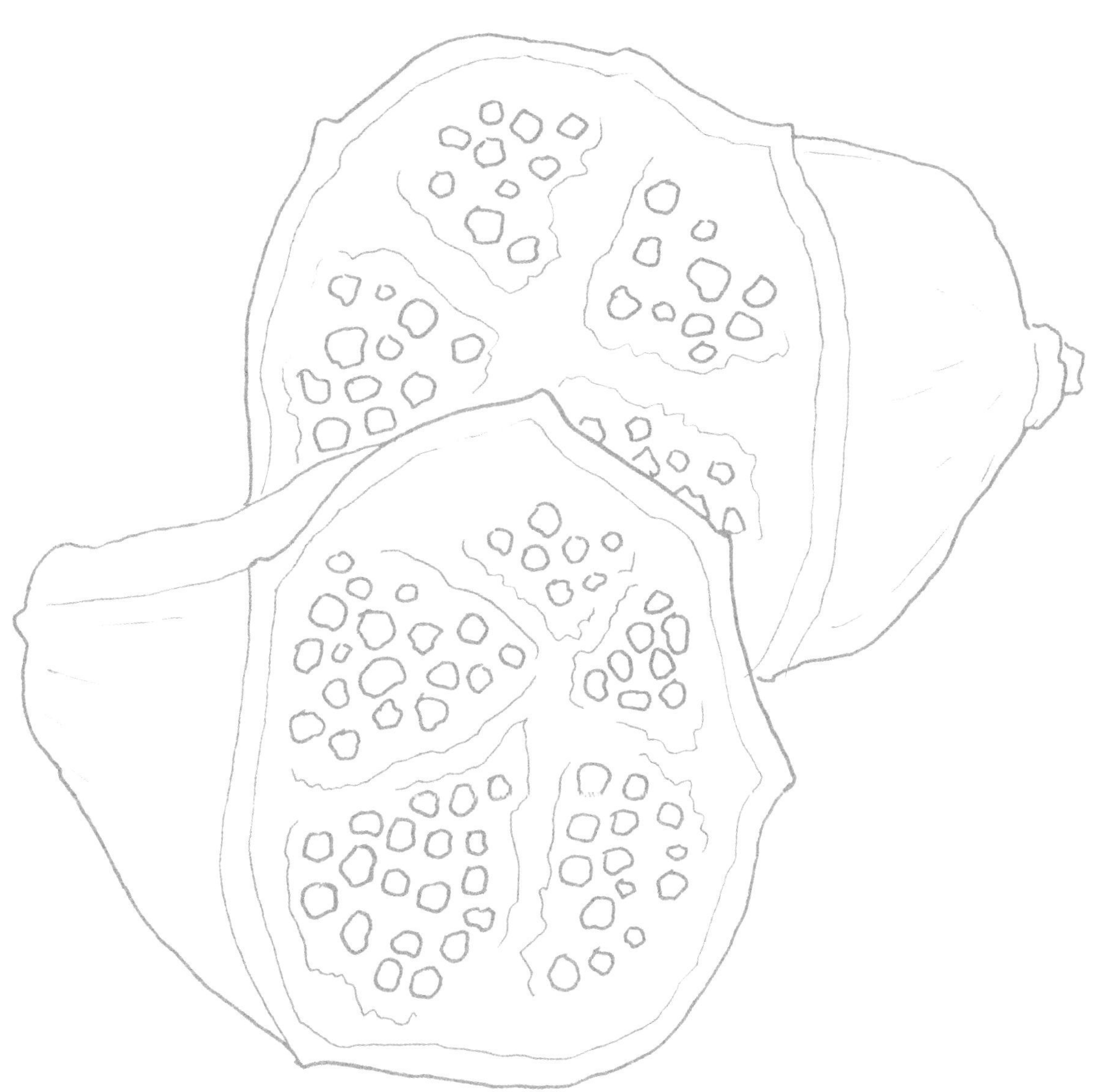

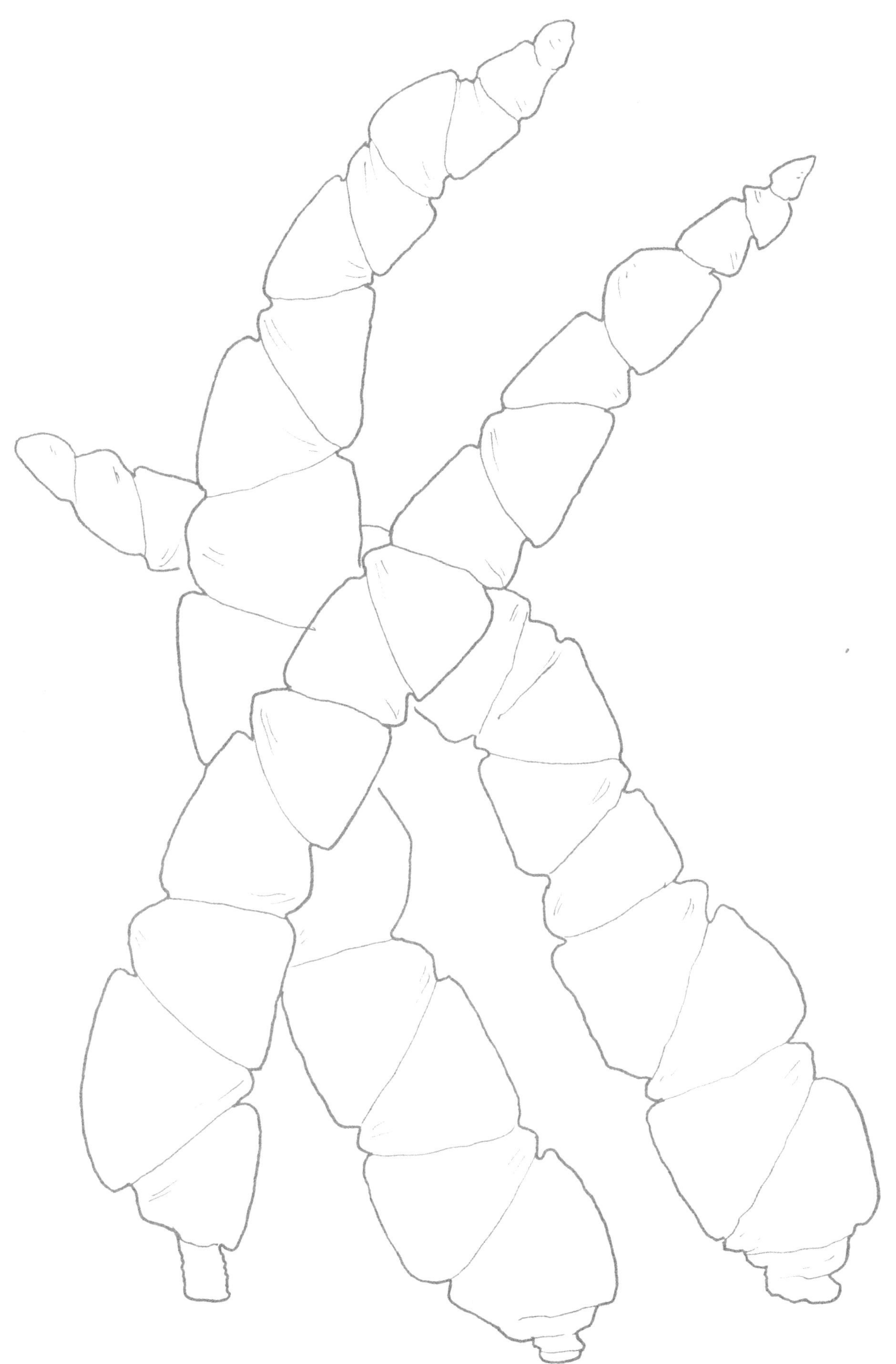

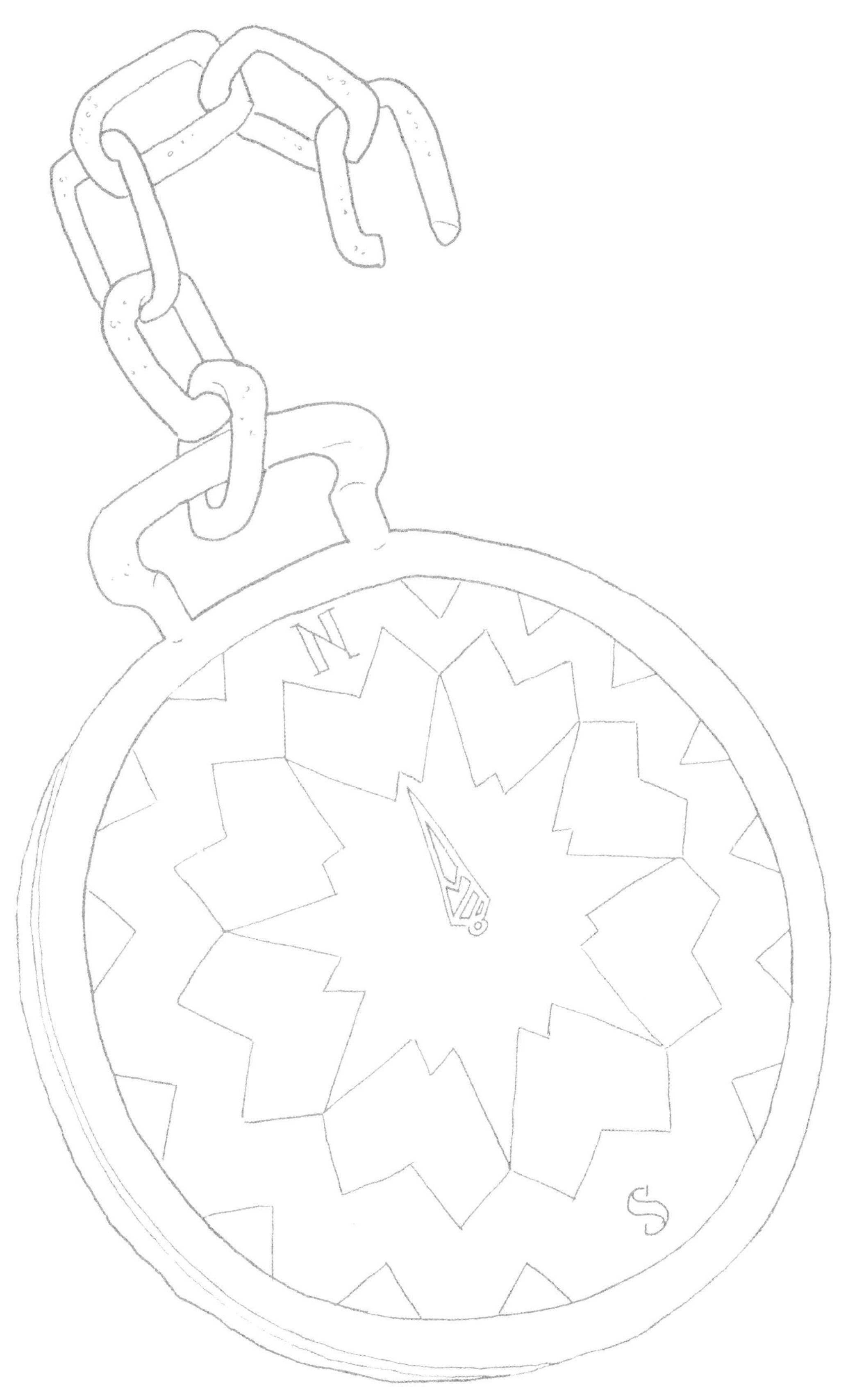
N
S

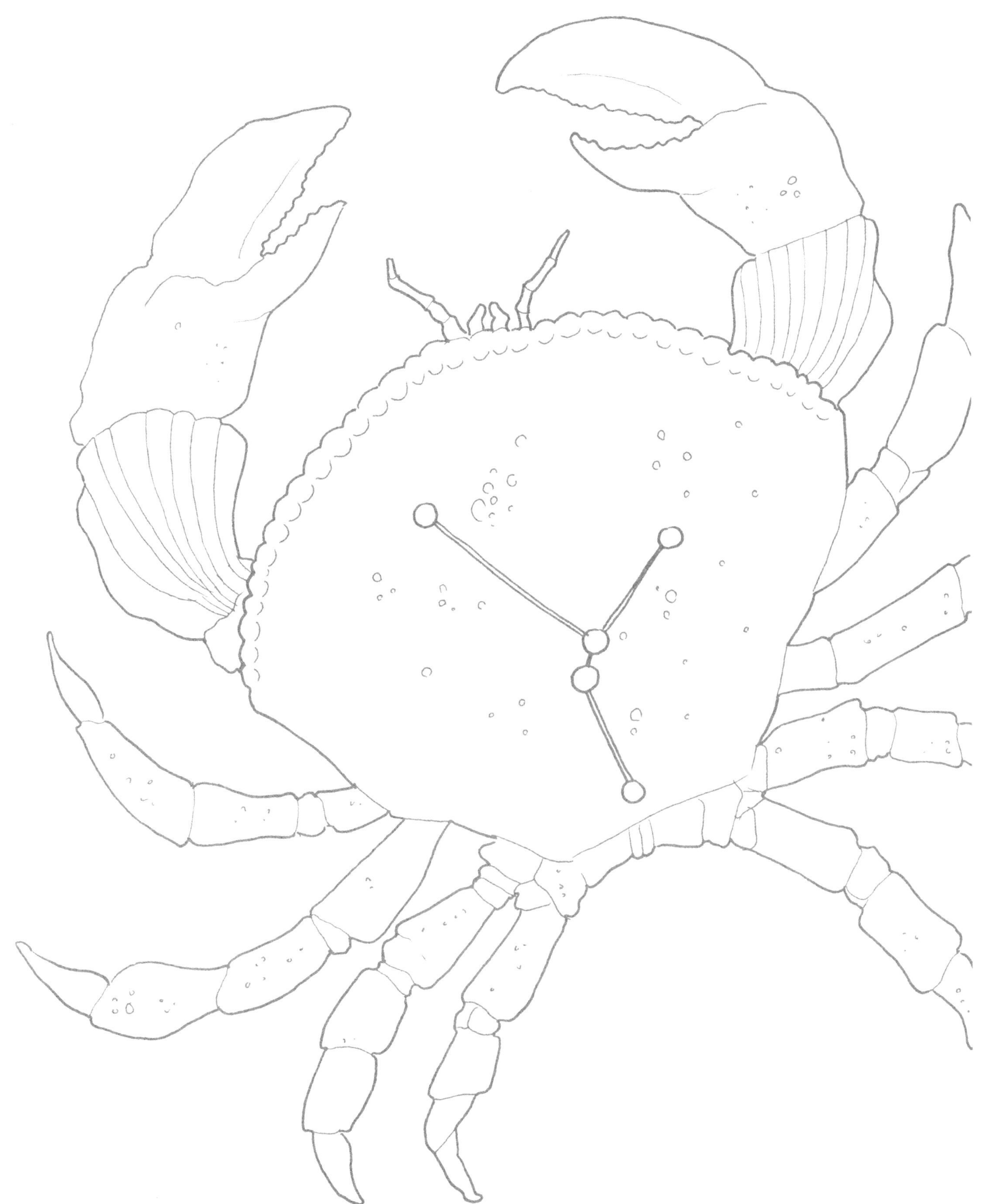

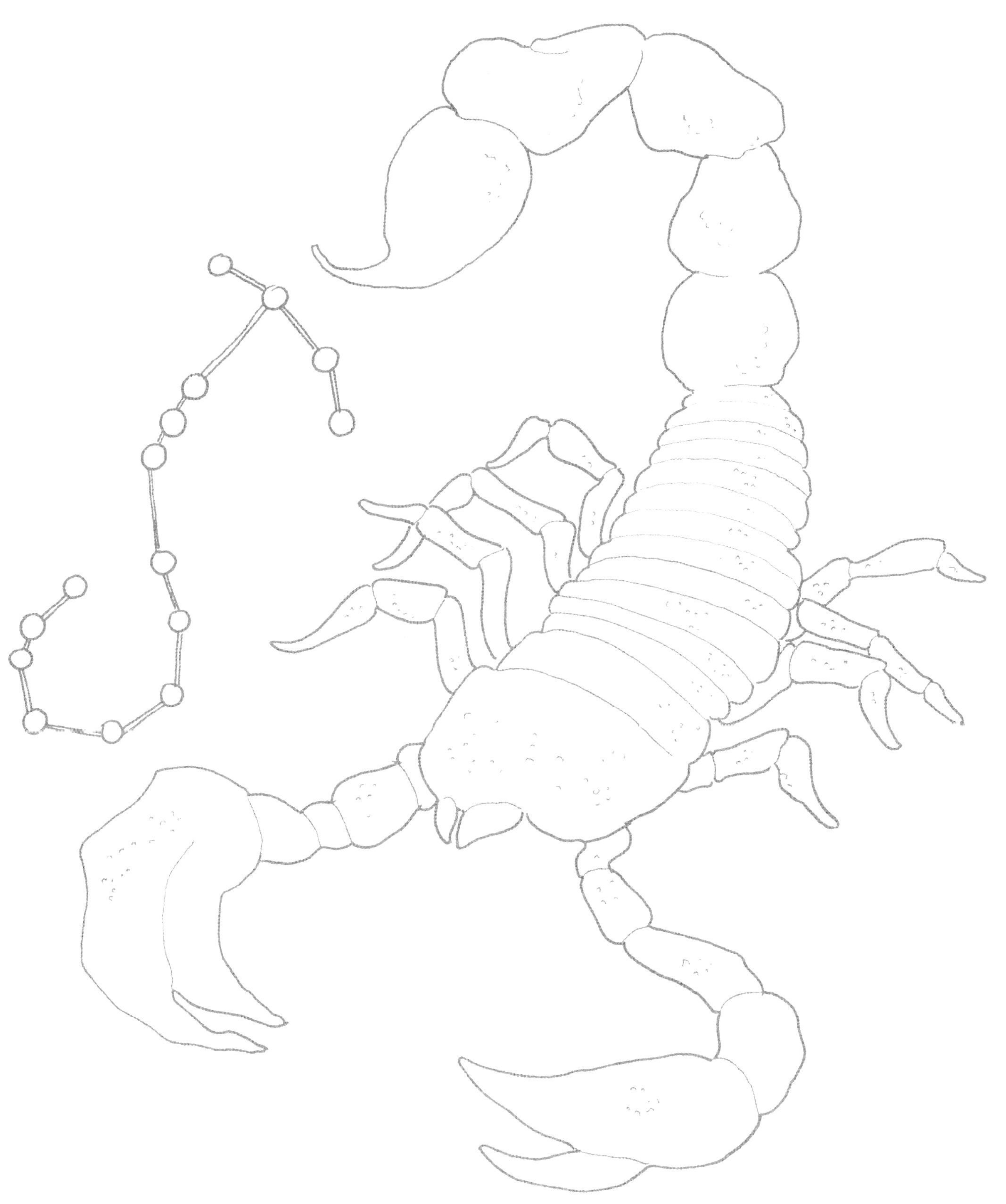

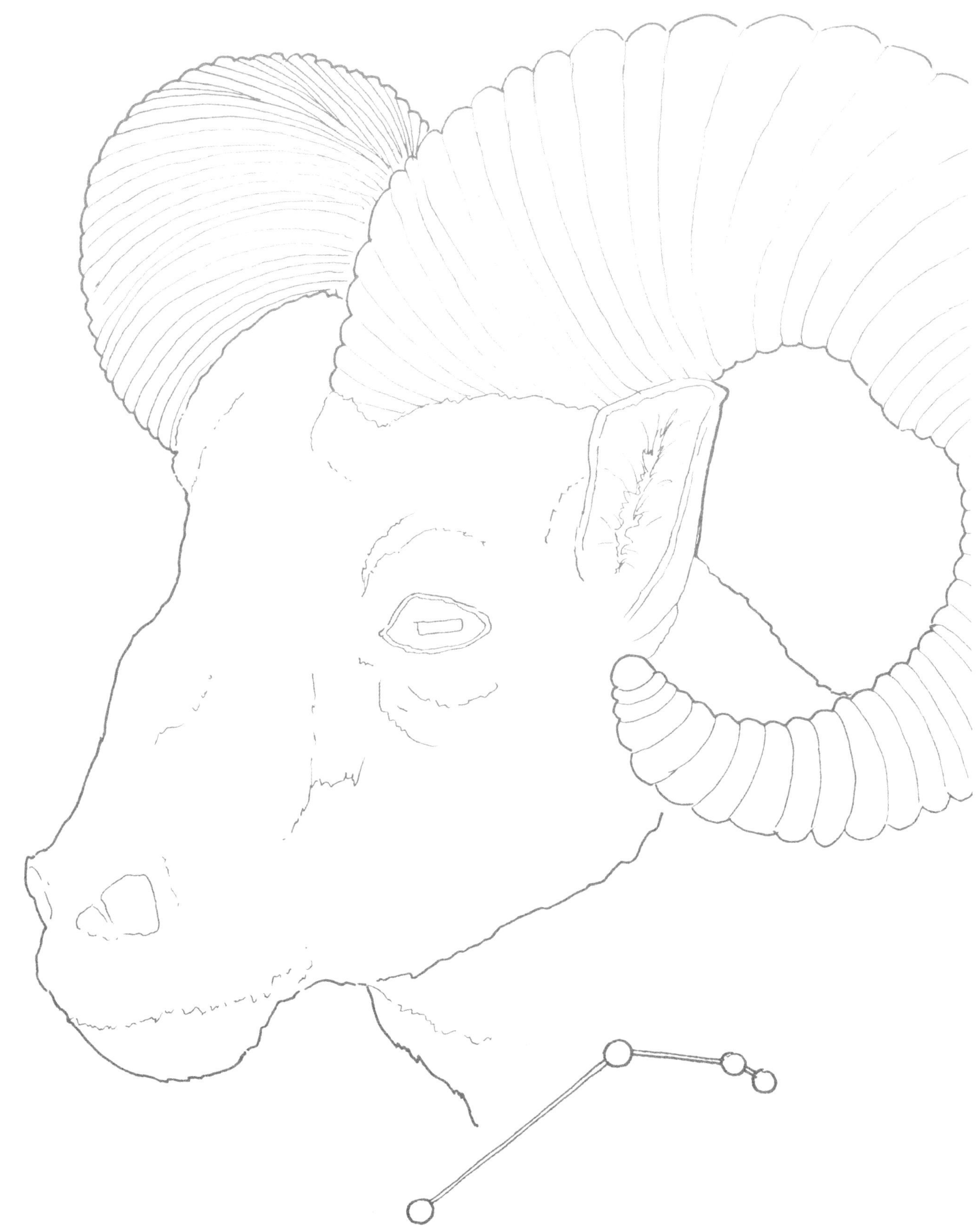

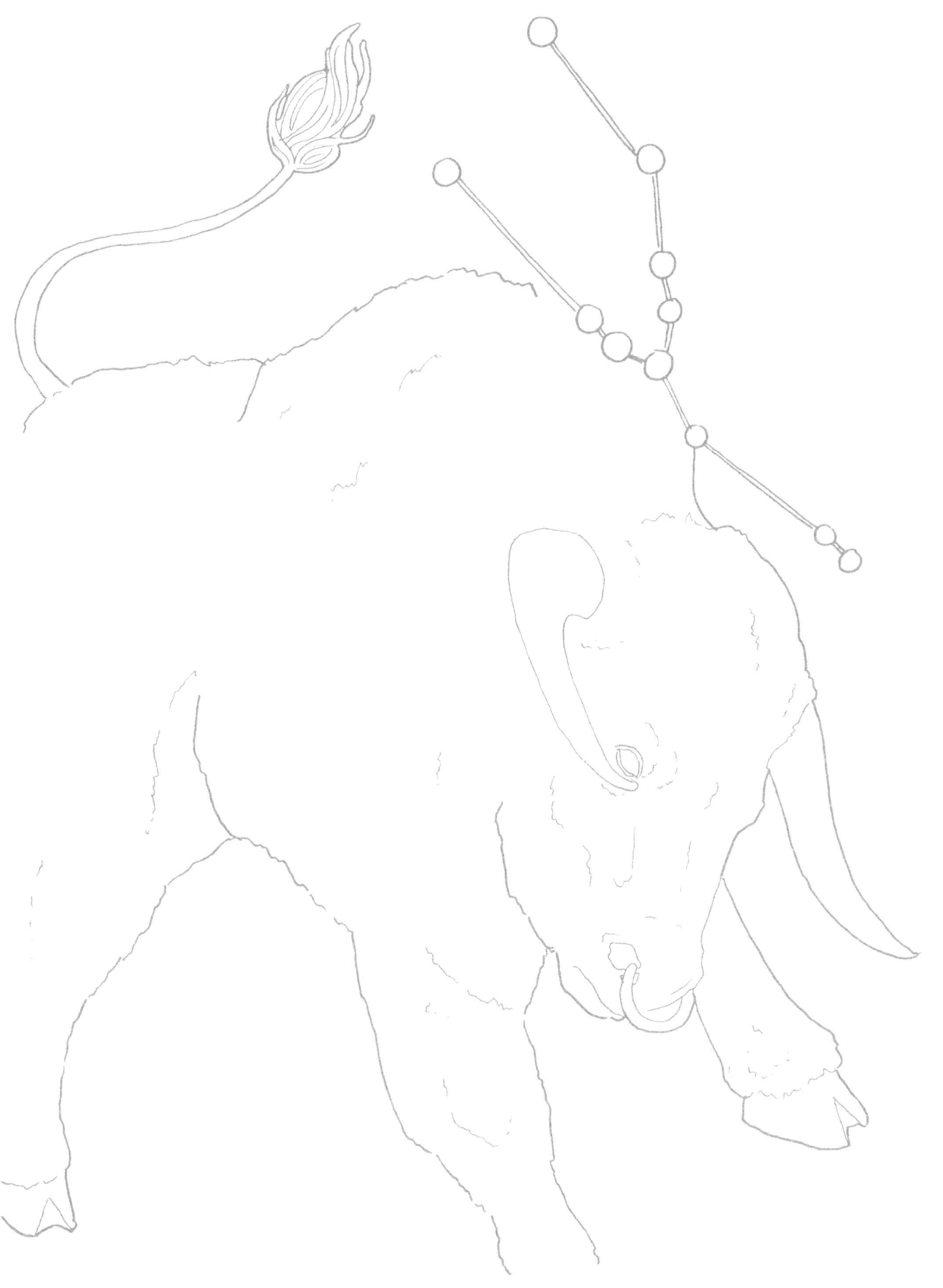

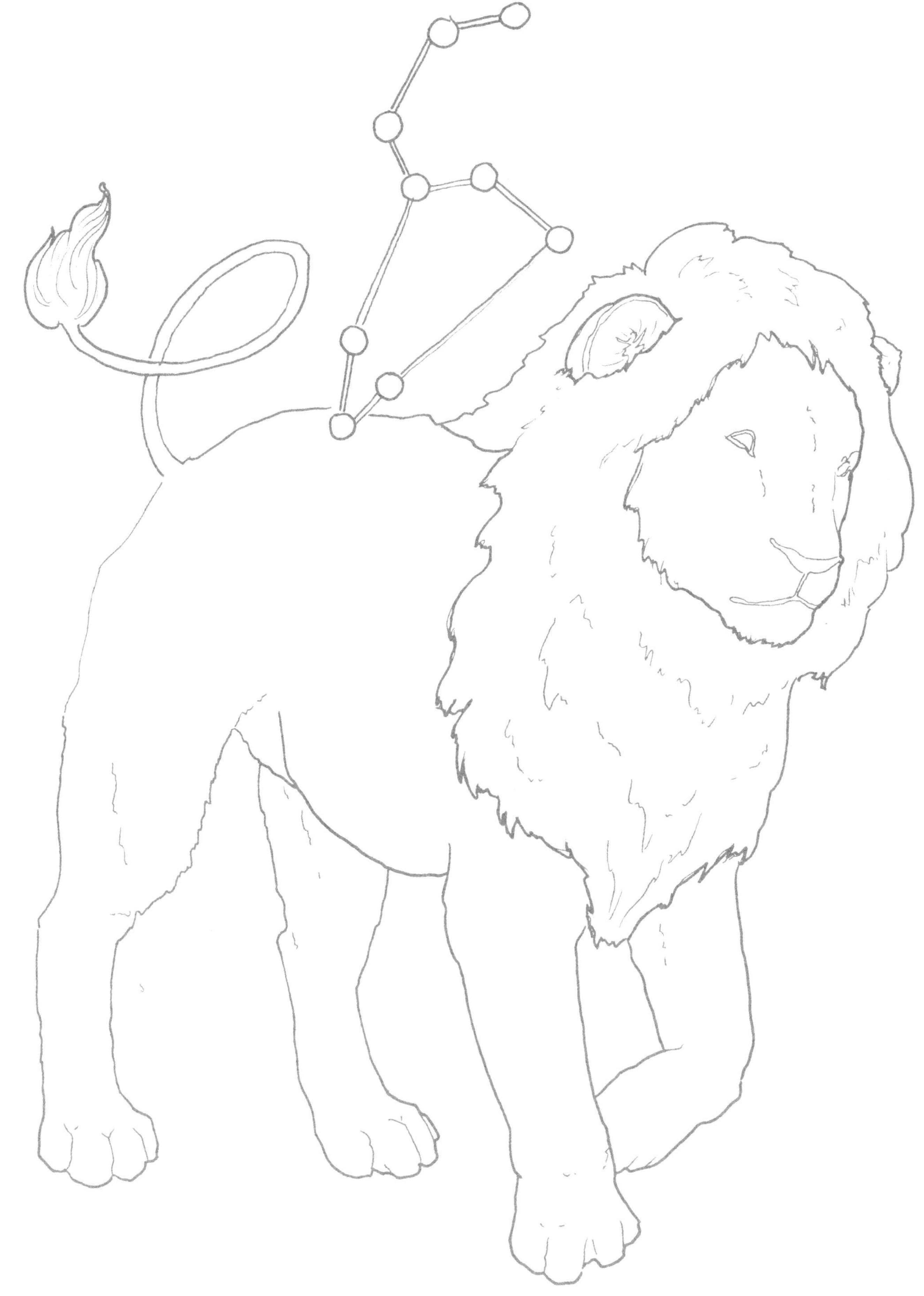

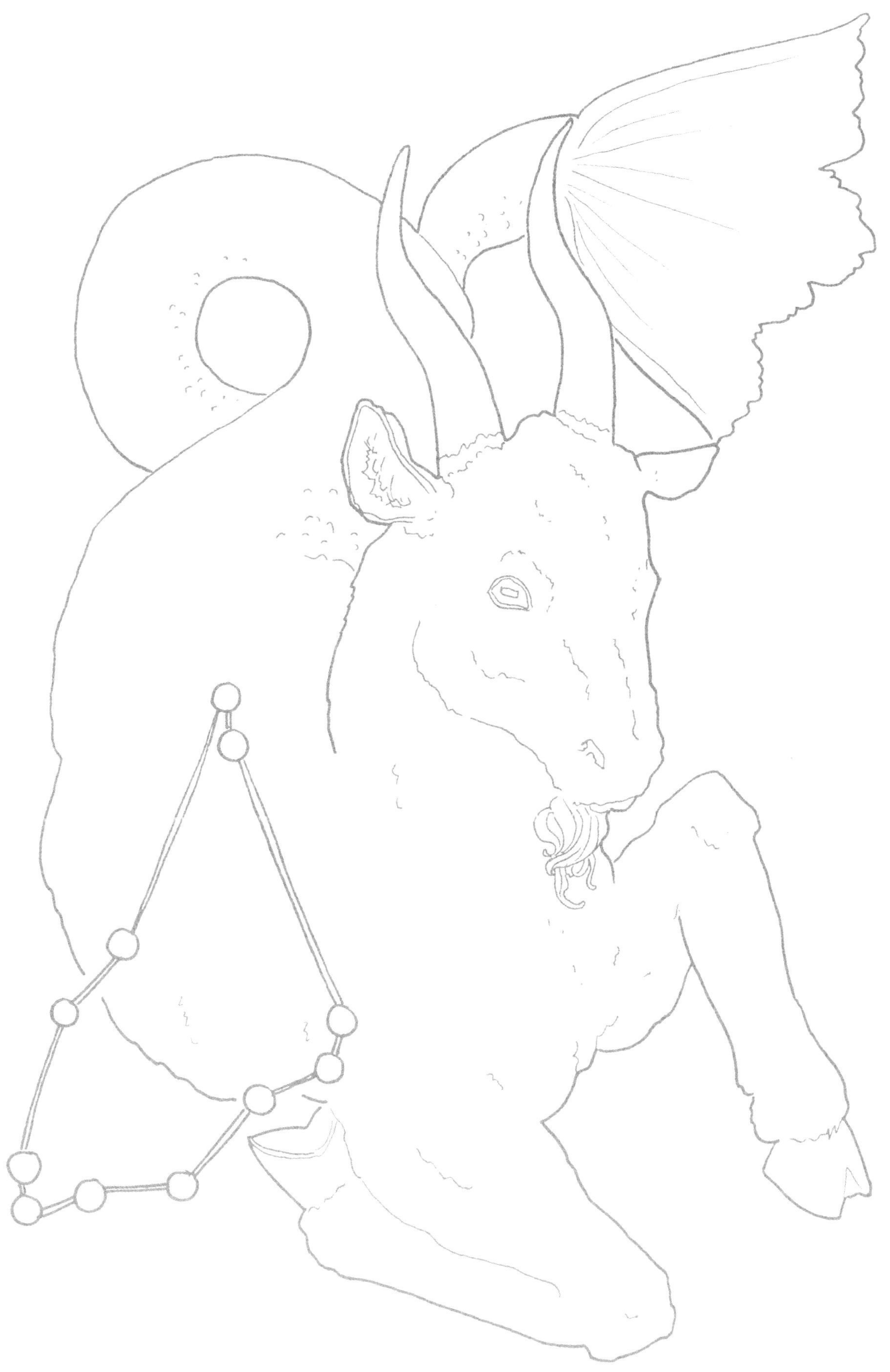

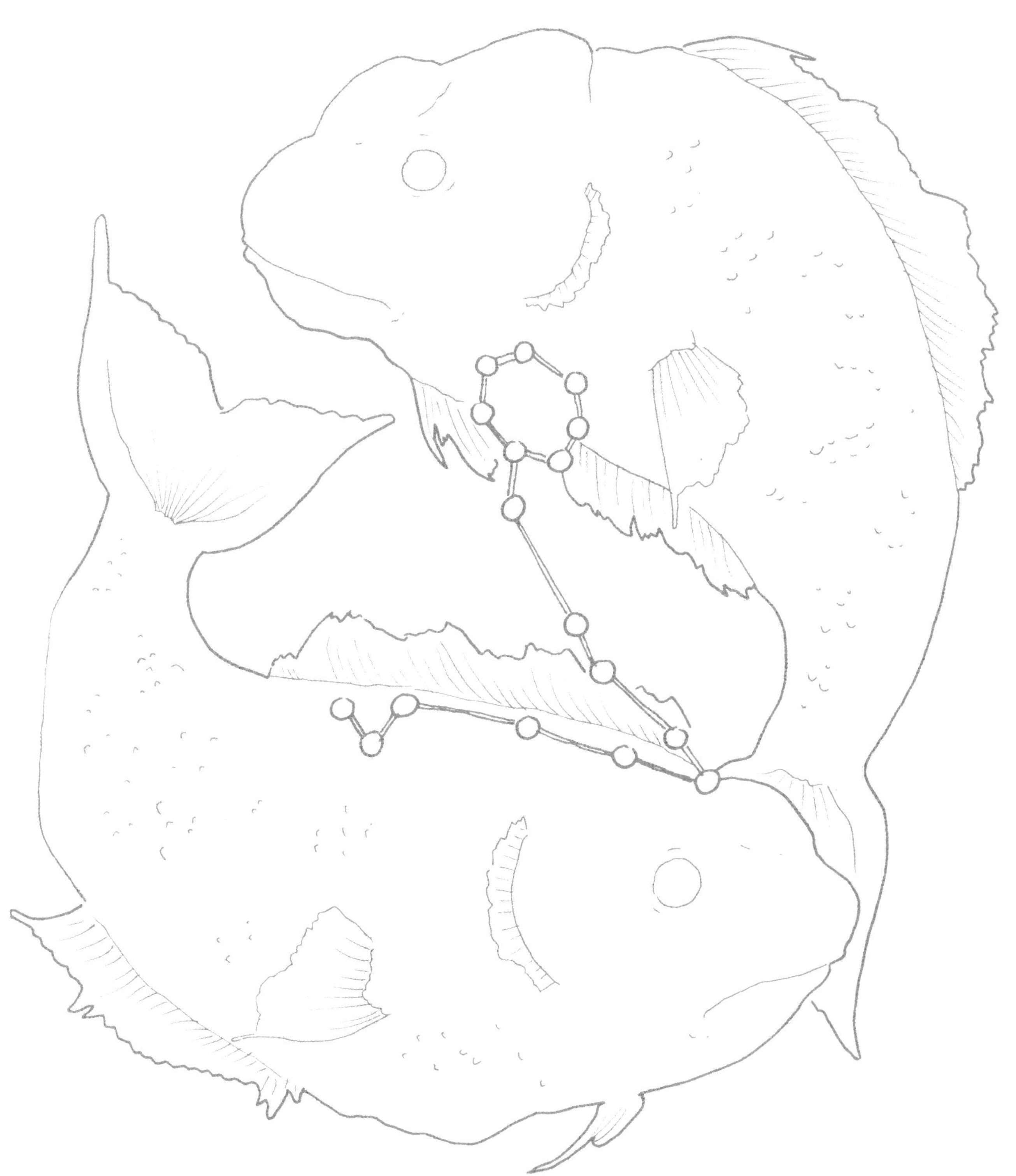

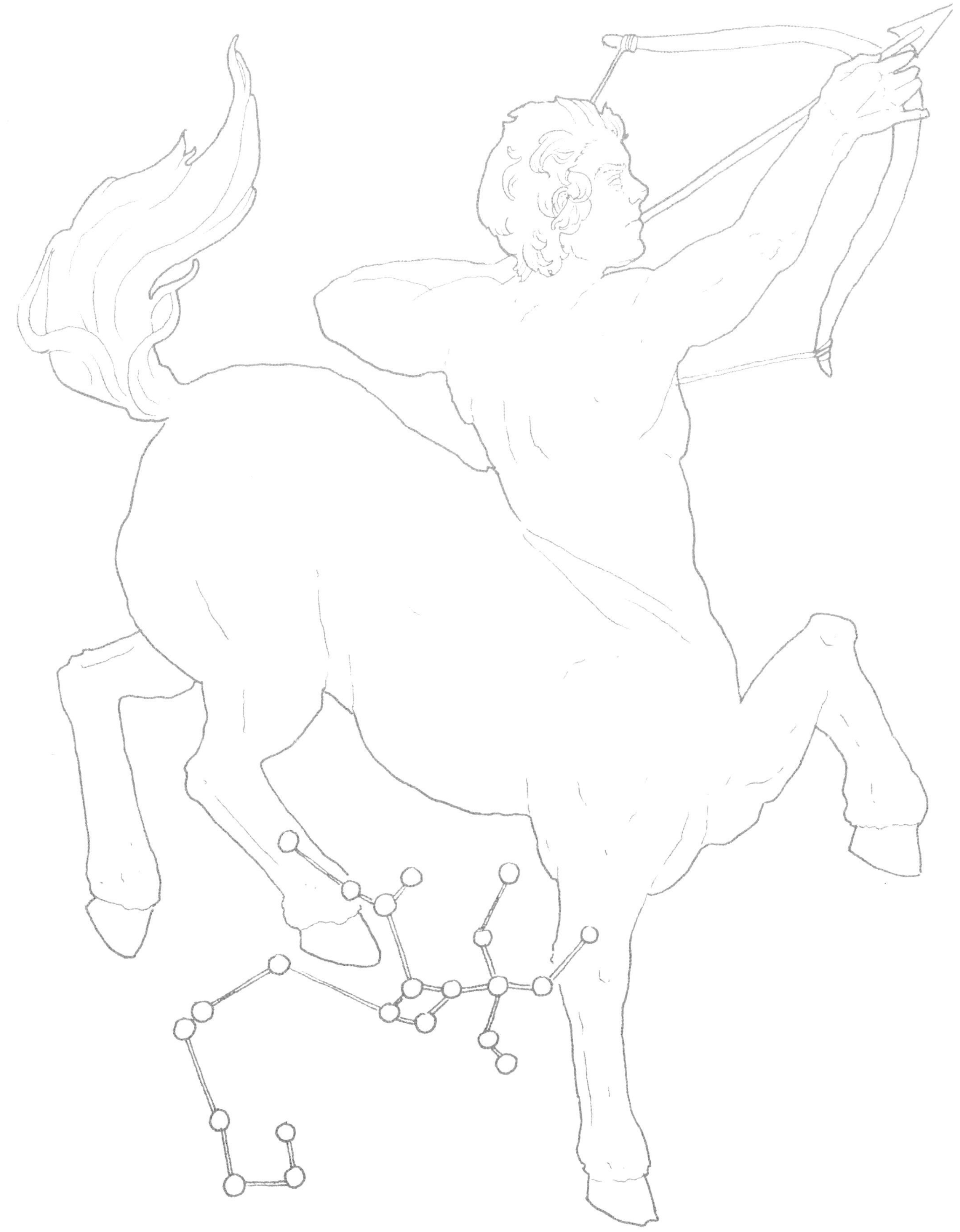

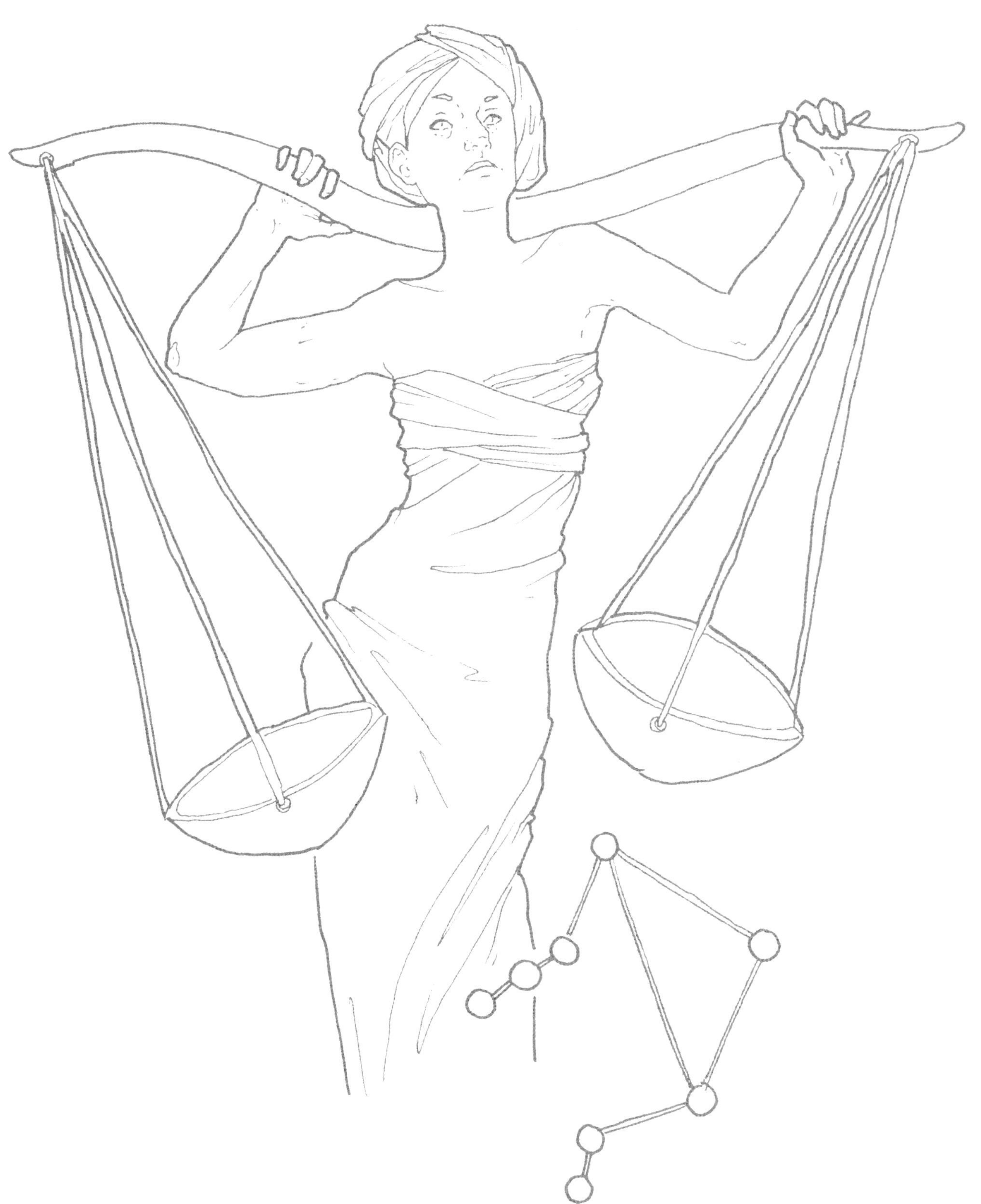

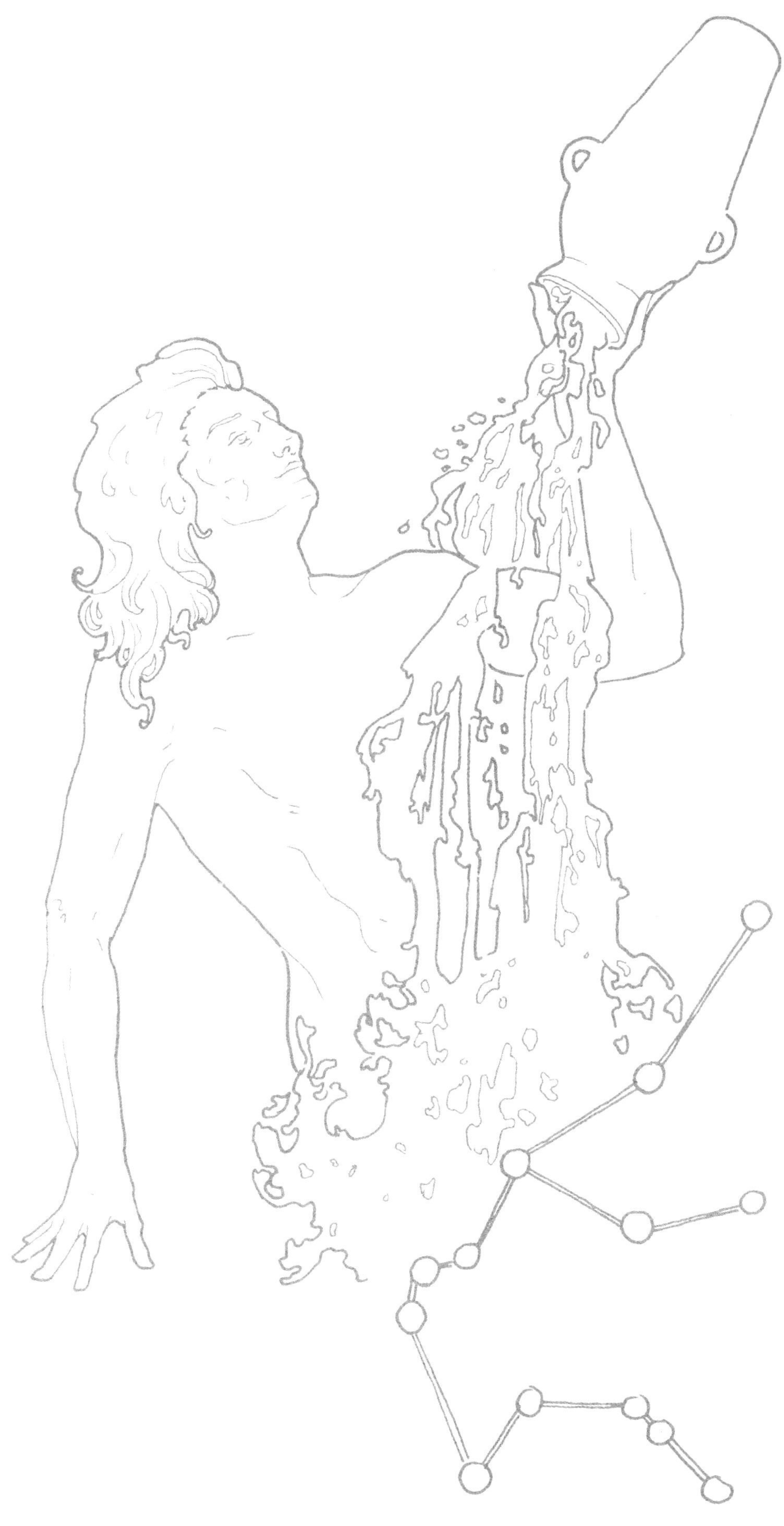

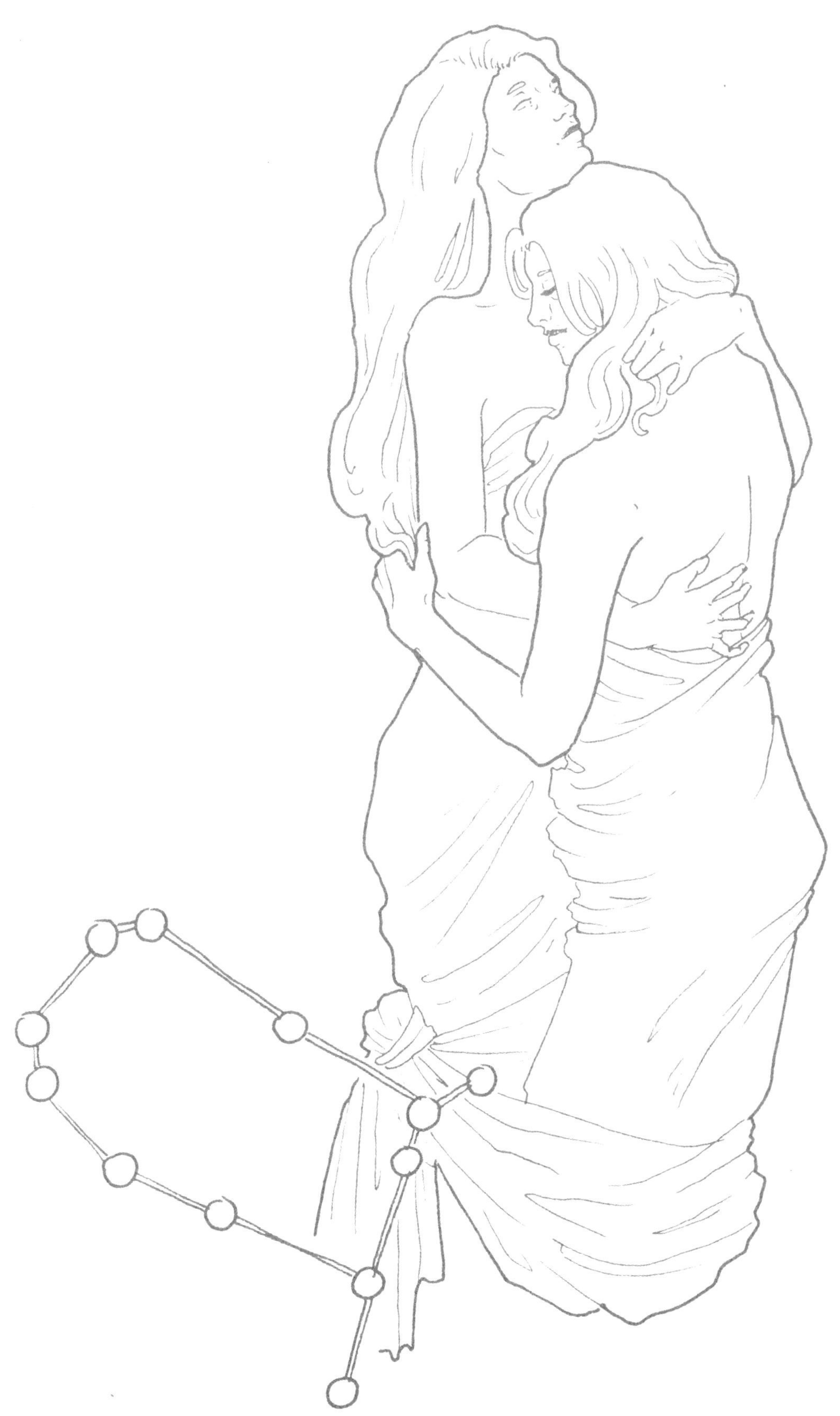

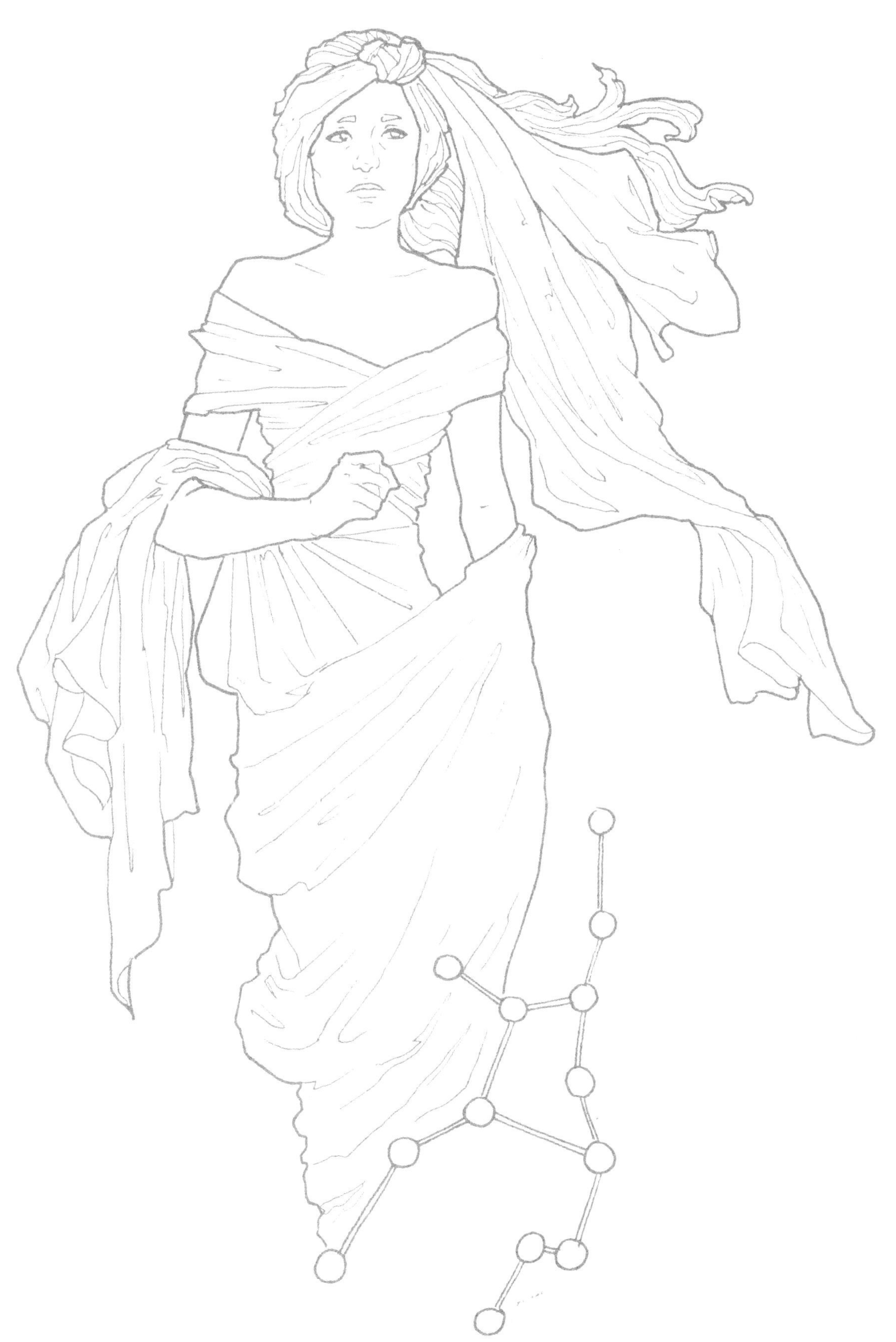

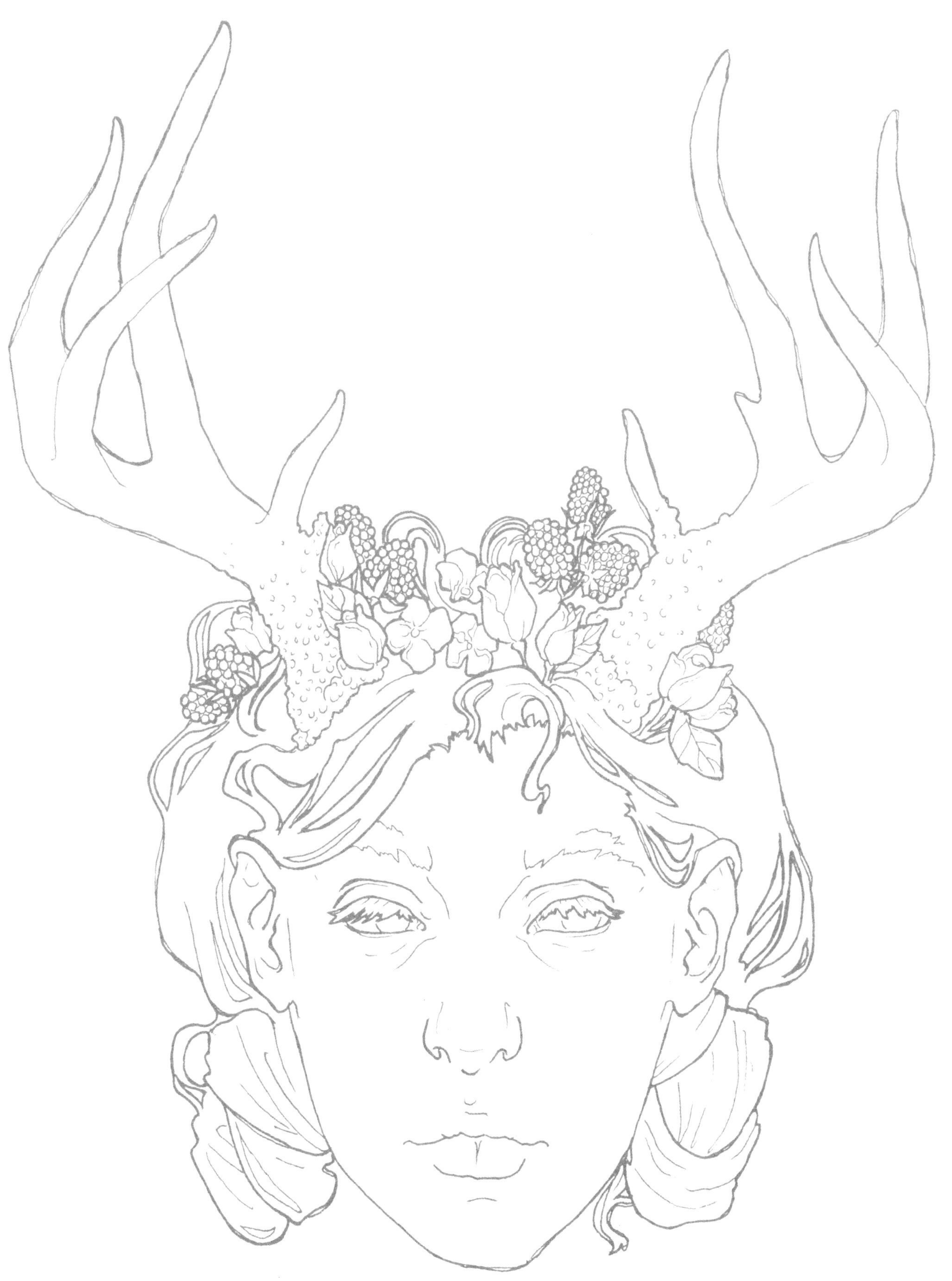

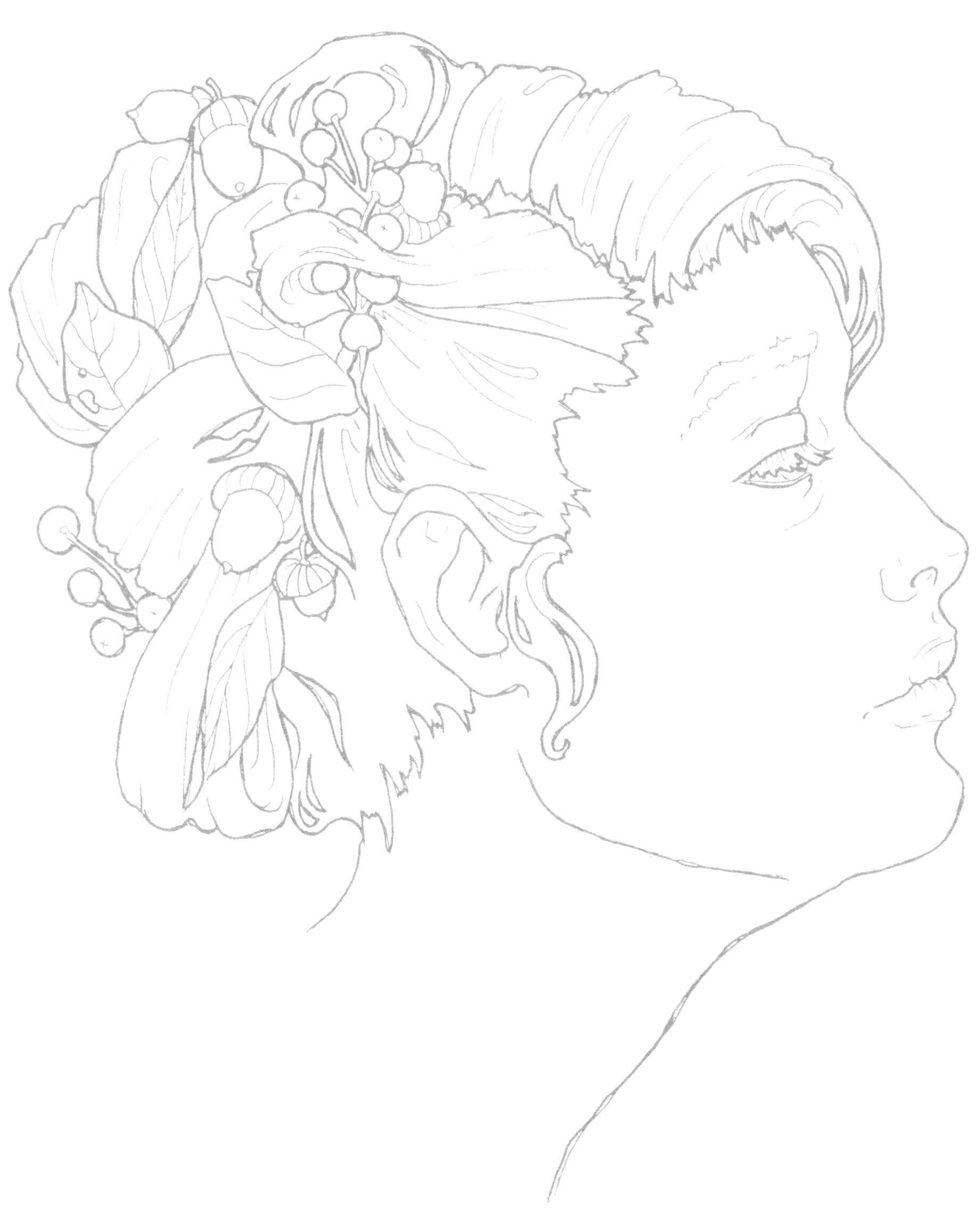

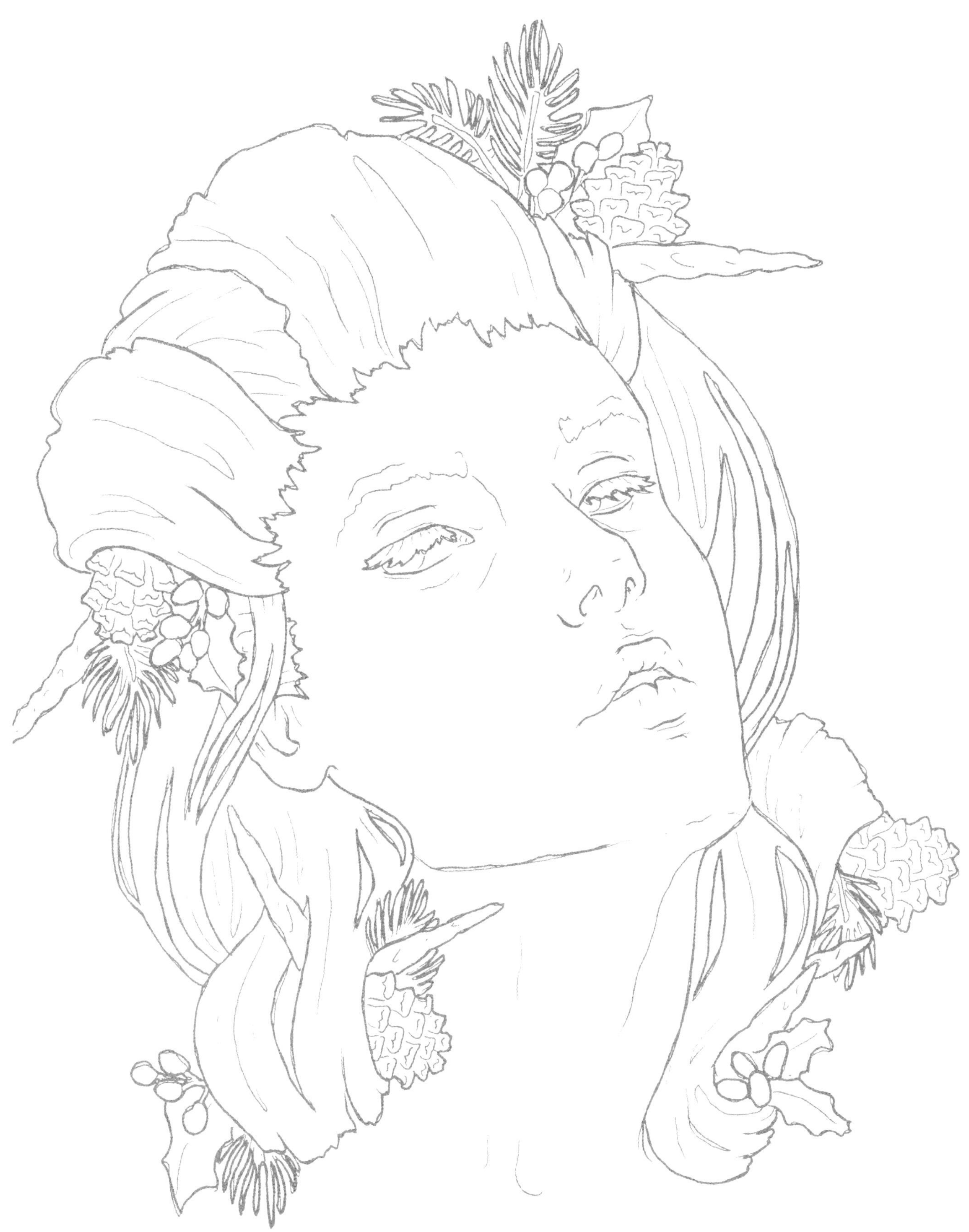

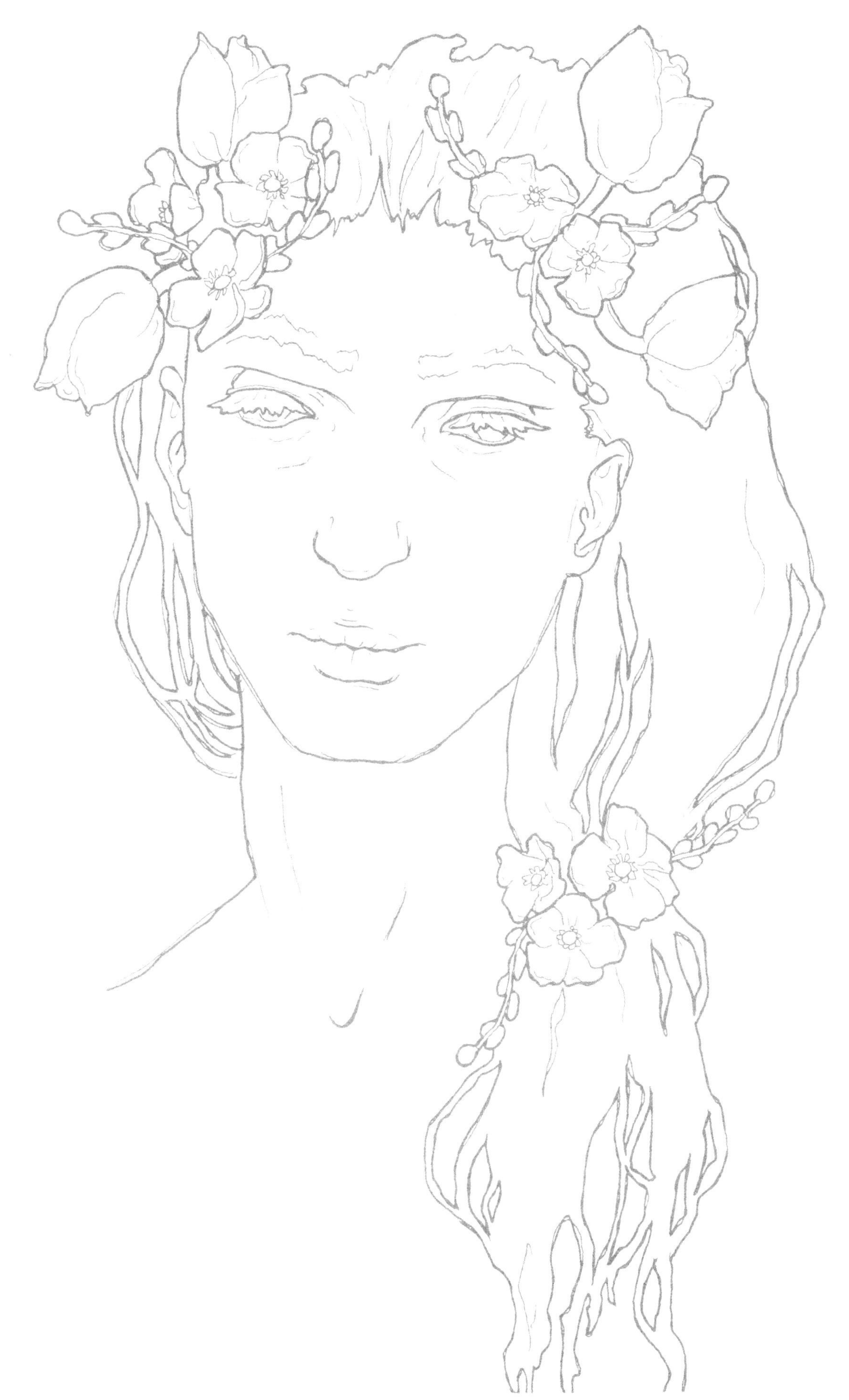

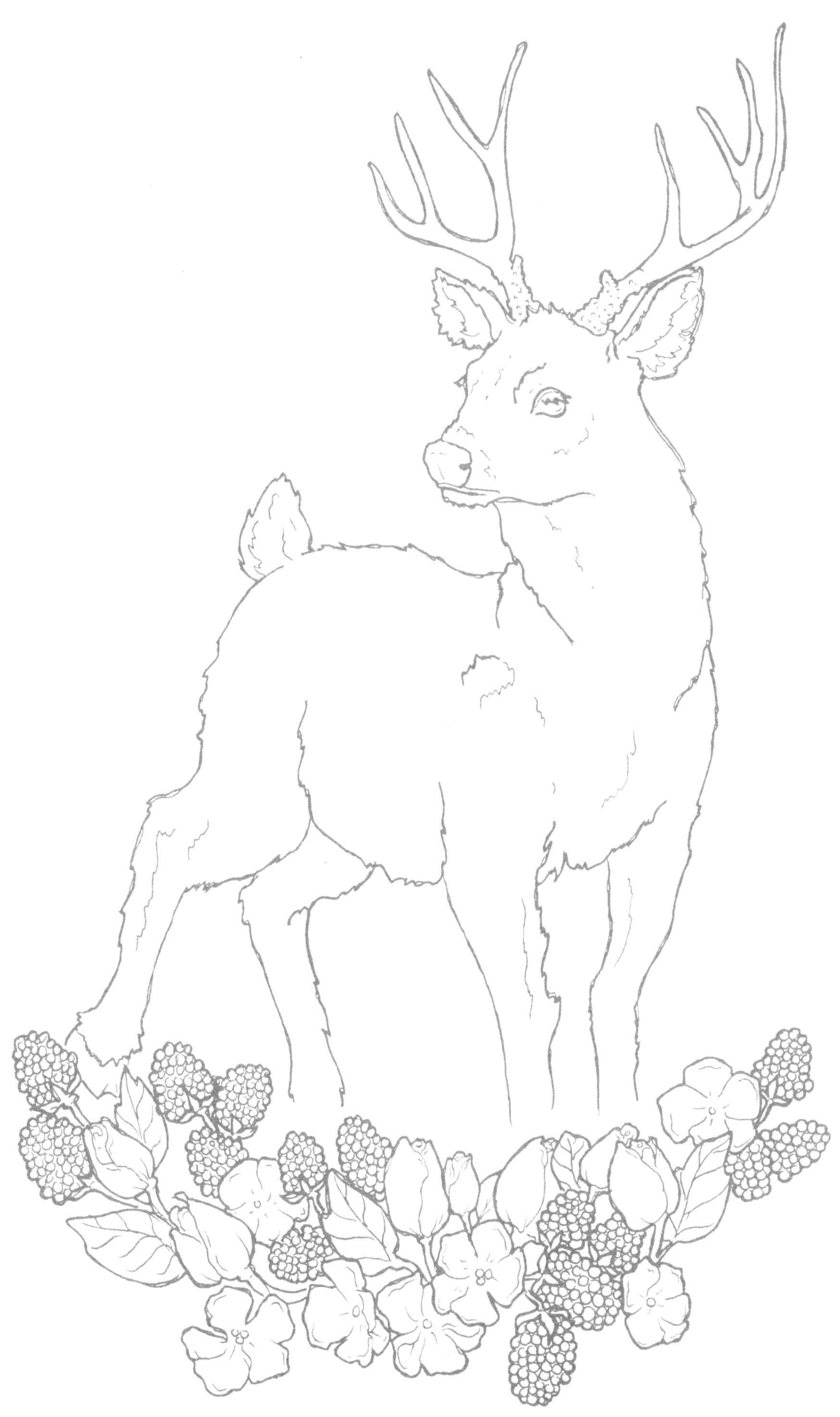

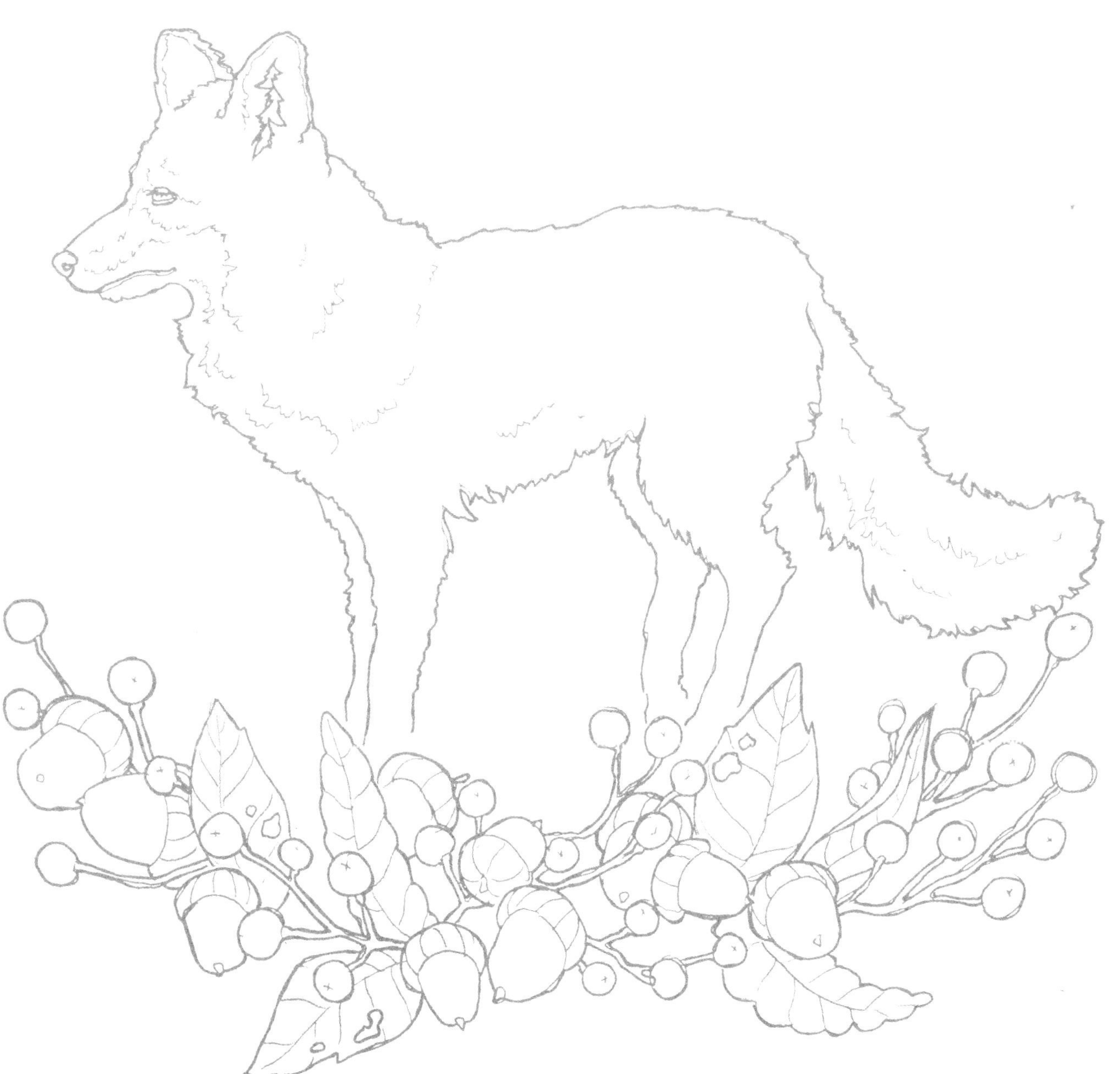

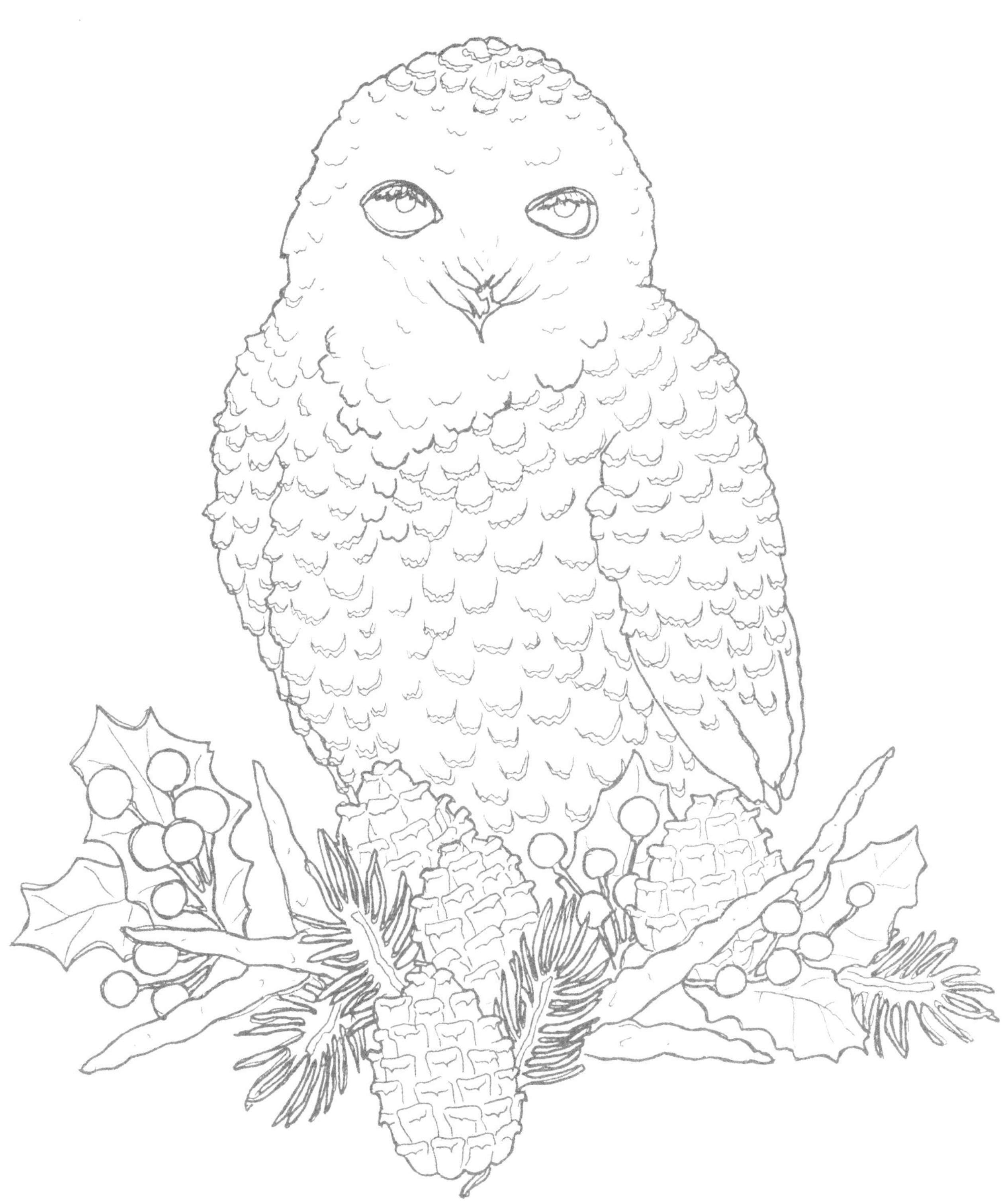

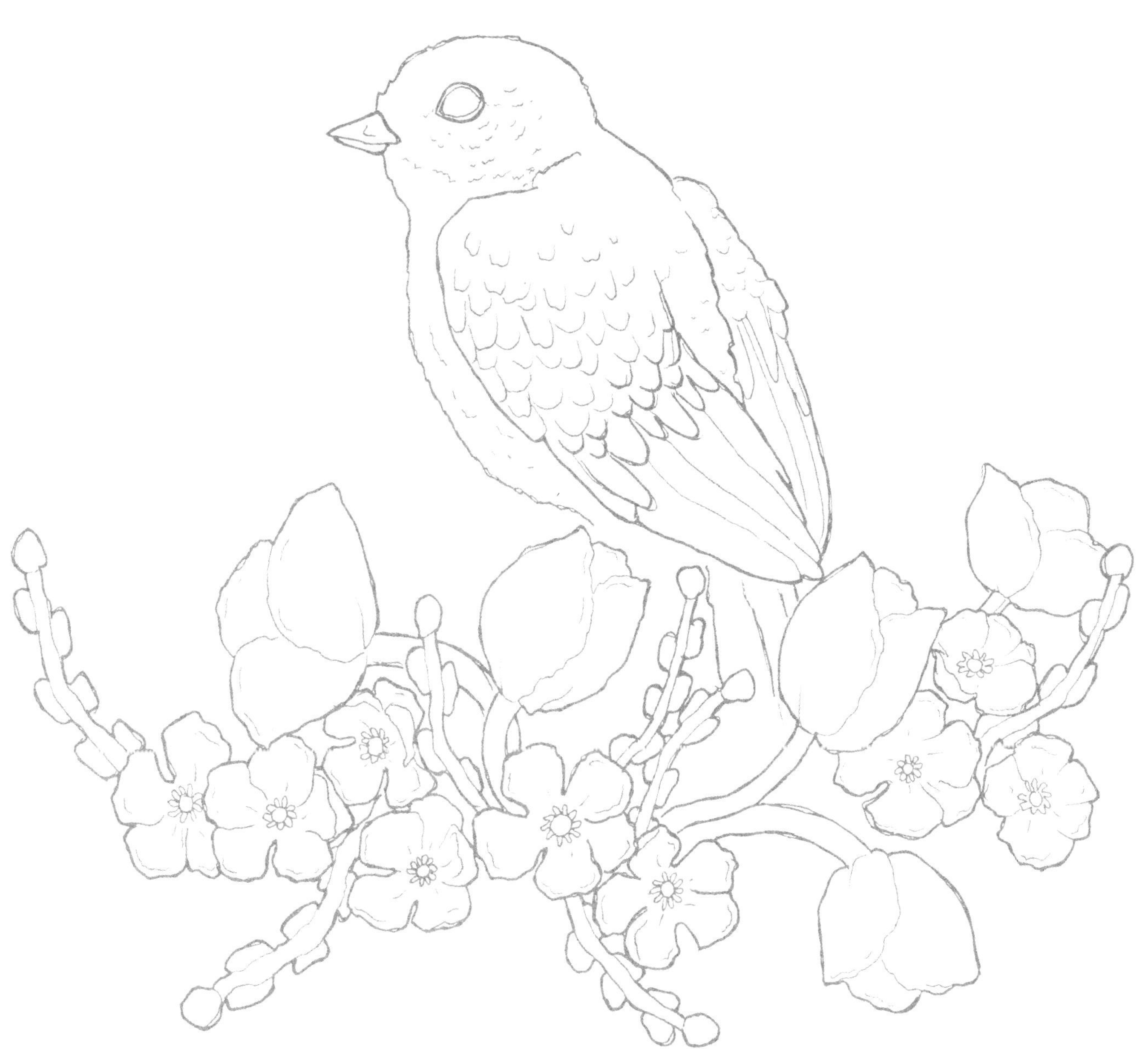

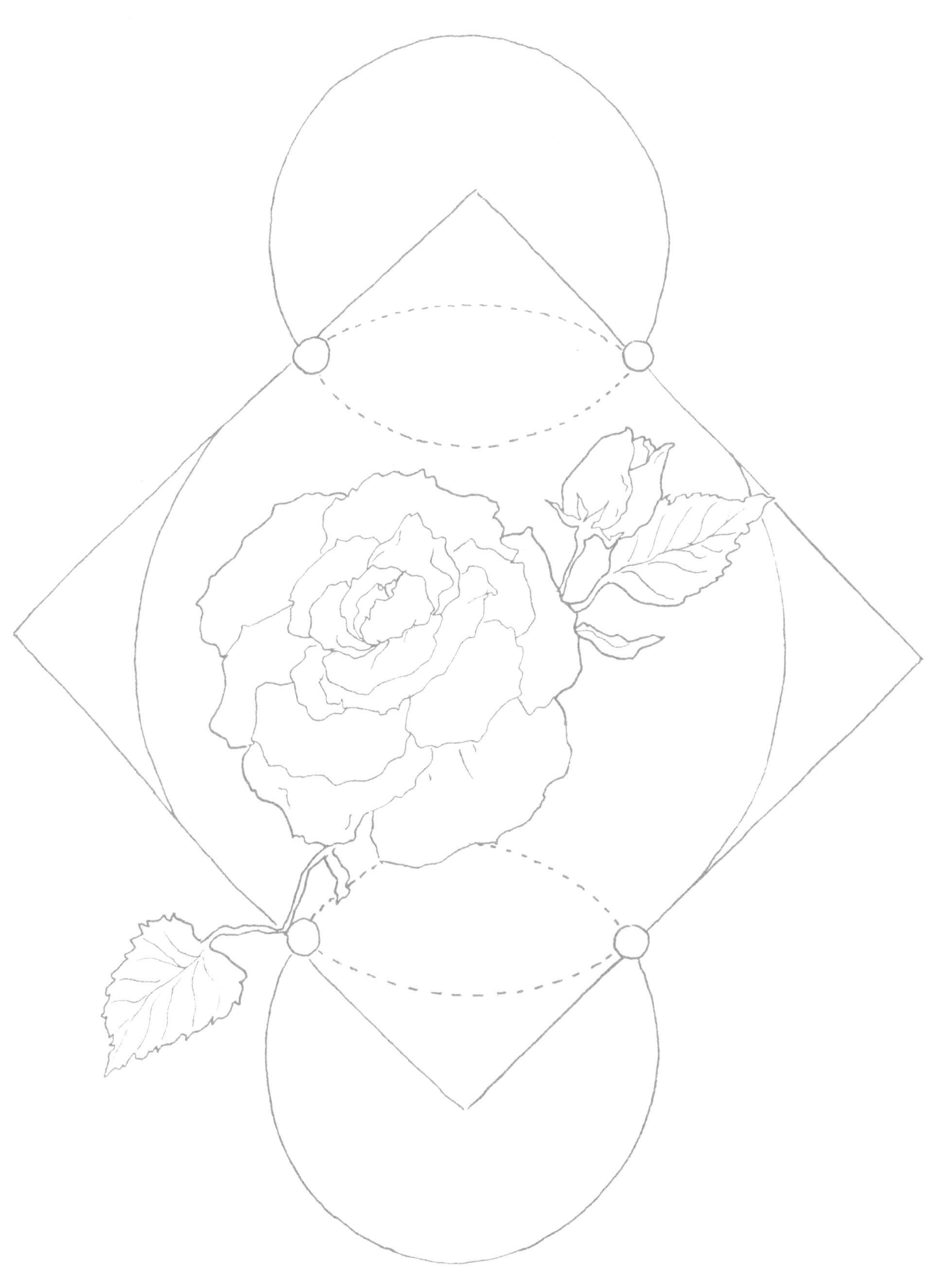

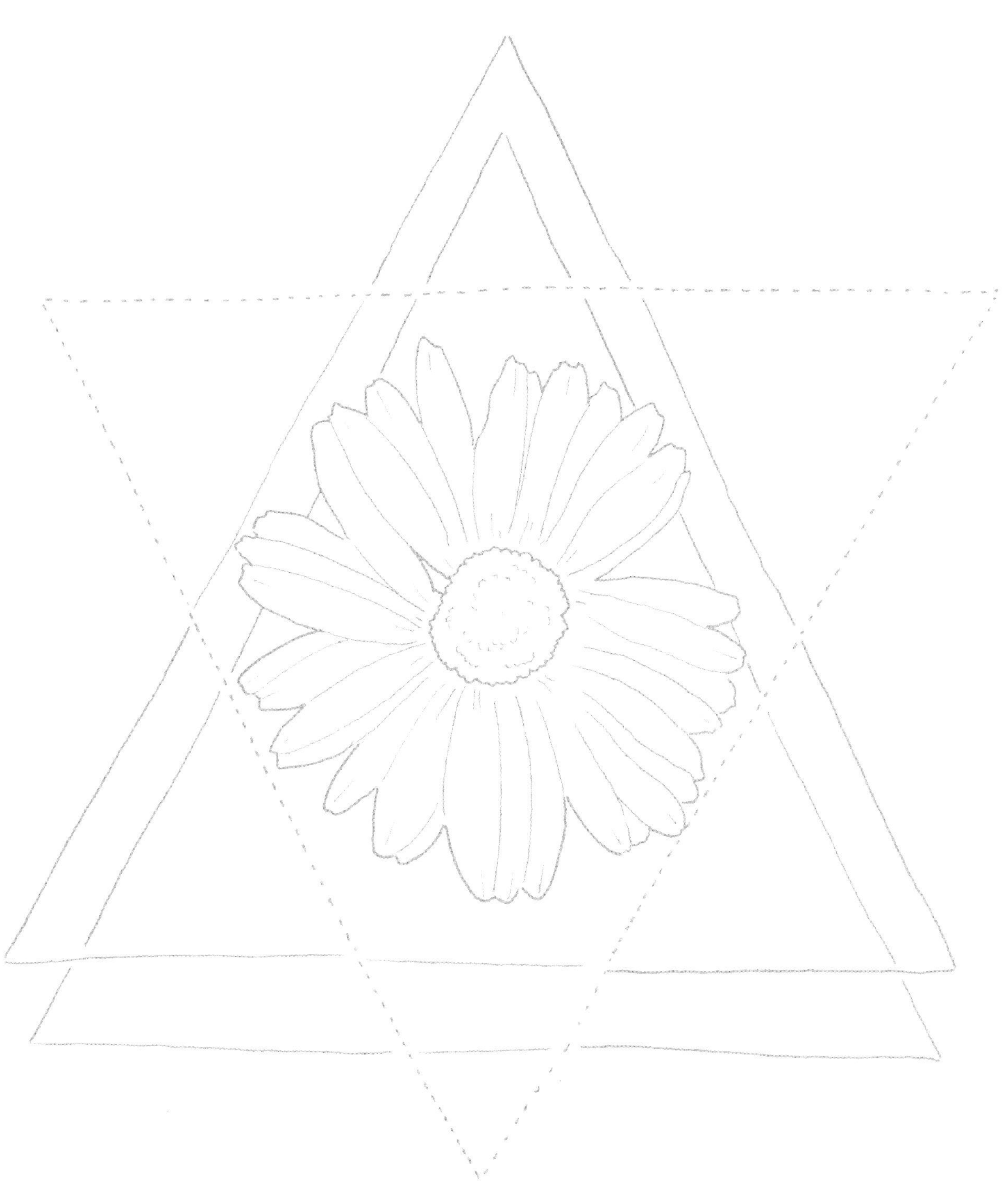

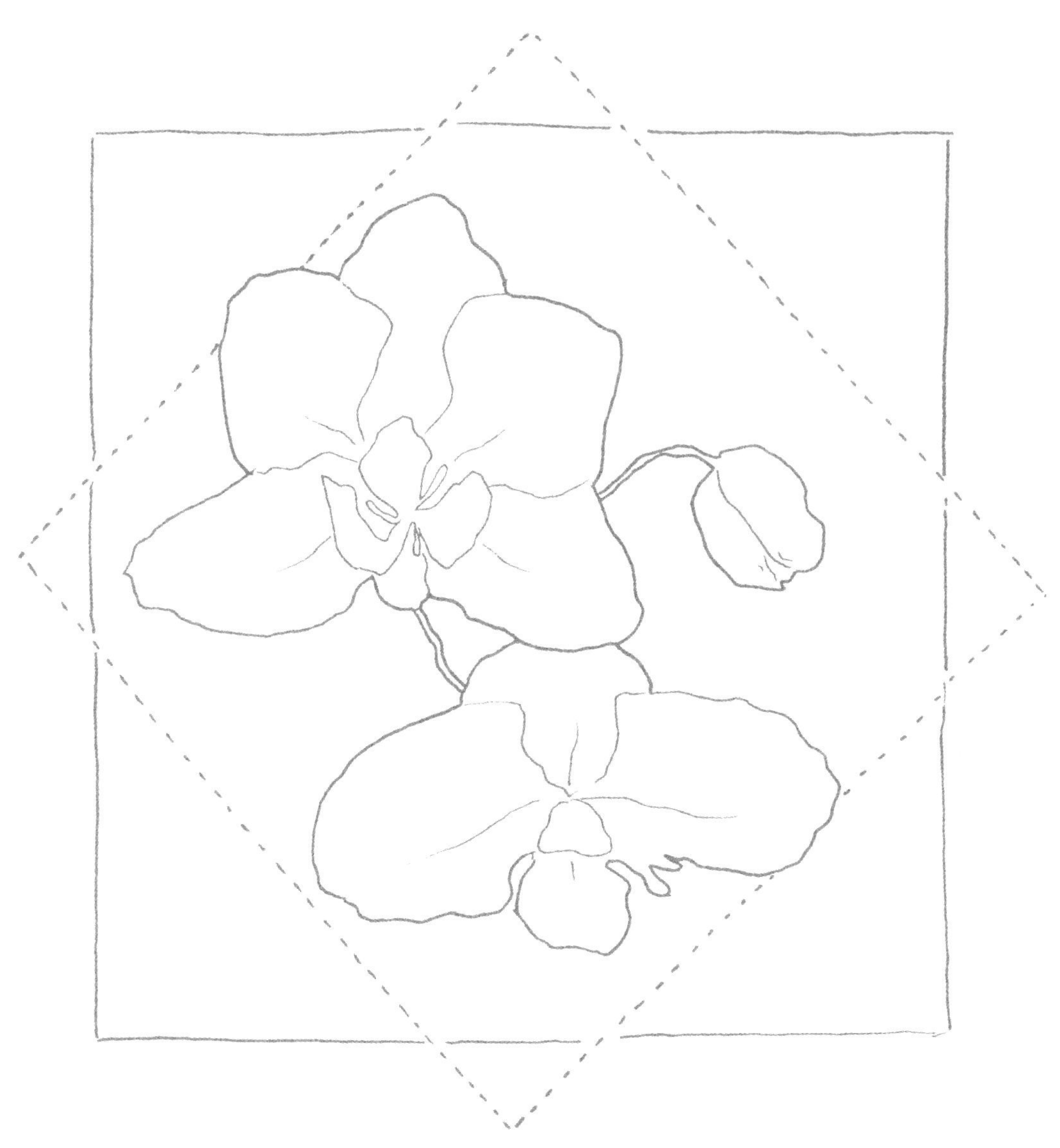

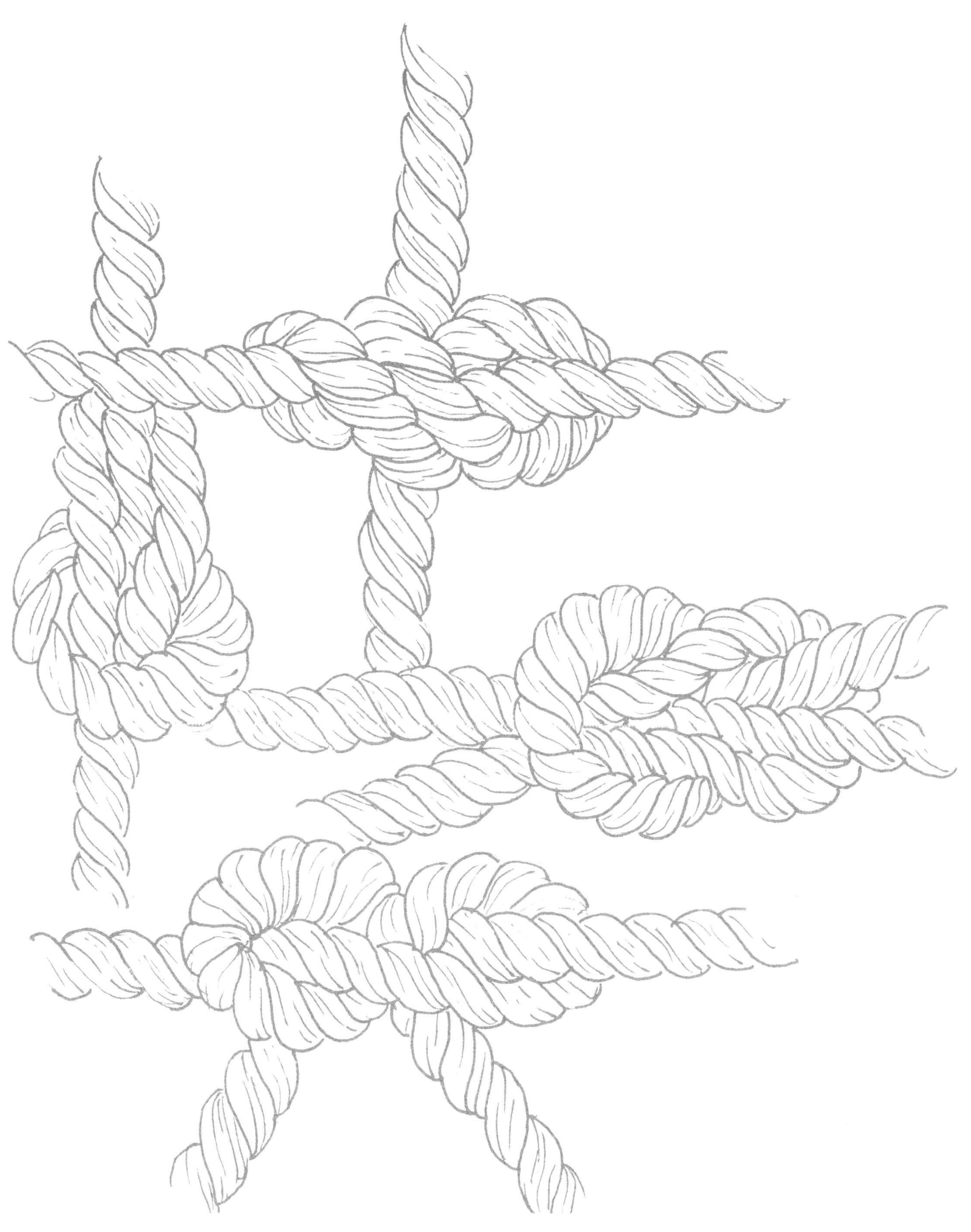

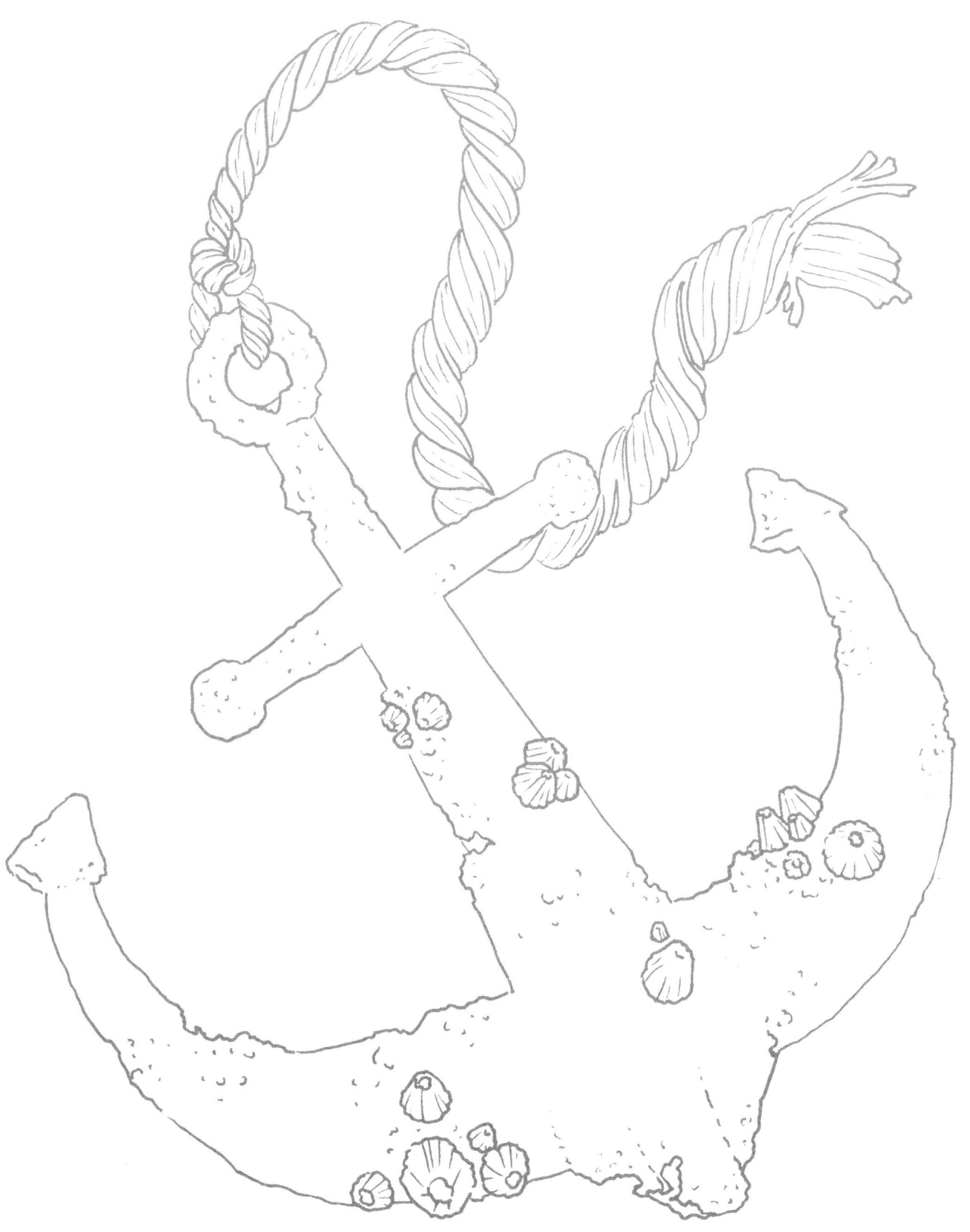

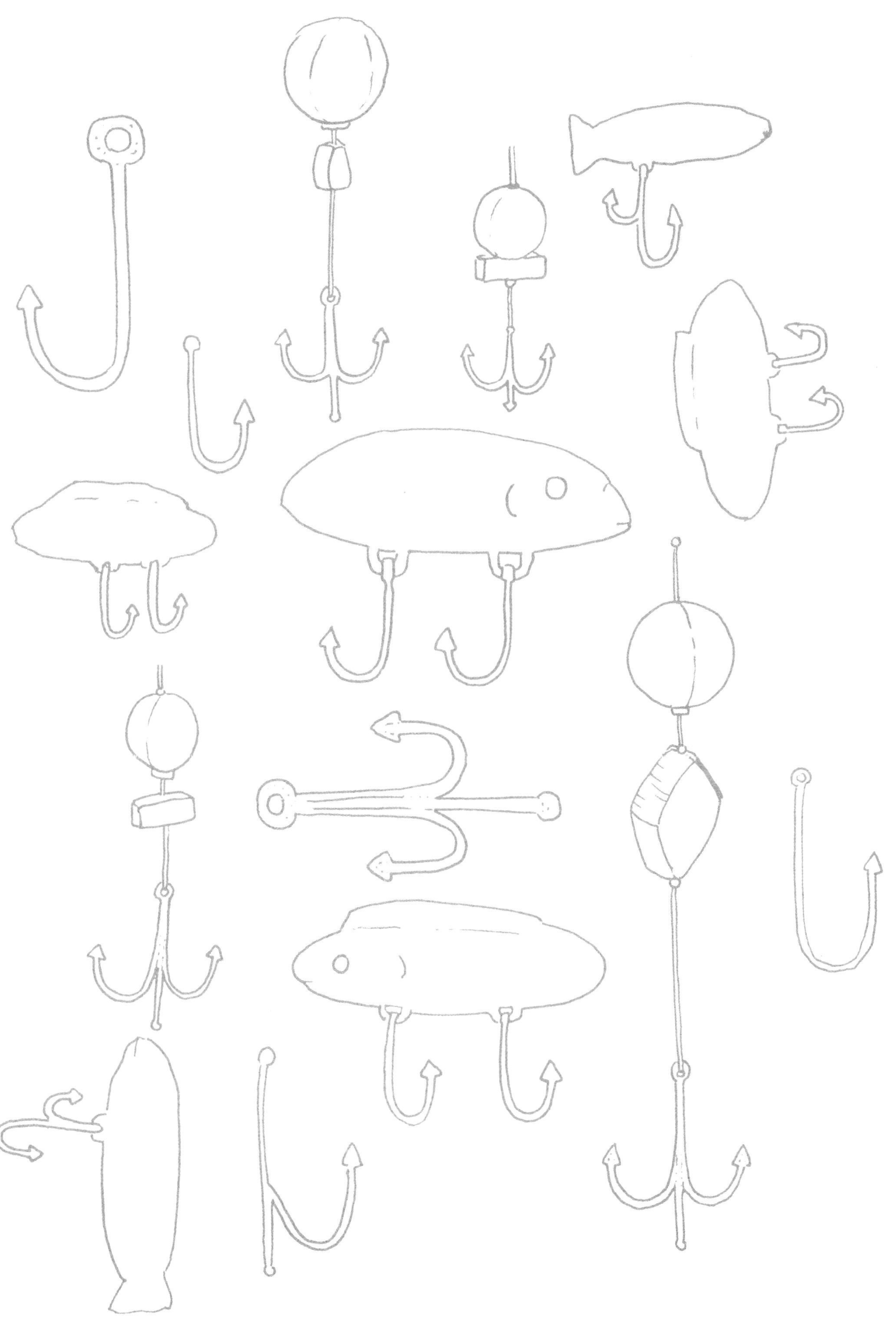